# Soul Stories
## how attachment shapes our lives

### By

# Hazel Leventhal

TSL Publications

Published in Great Britain in 2020
By TSL Publications, Rickmansworth

Copyright © 2020 Hazel Leventhal

ISBN: 978-1-913294-50-2

# Contents

# Introduction

This book is a combination of personal memoirs and psychotherapy case studies from an attachment-based perspective. I felt prompted to write it because whenever I read work on psychotherapy I always find the little vignettes or snippets fascinating and want to know more about what happened. That is why I decided to include case studies that follow a therapy from beginning to end, in greatly condensed form.

These case studies are all true stories and the people involved have given permission for their inclusion. However, the names and other details have been changed. I also thought that readers might be interested to understand why I chose to become an attachment-based psychotherapist, and so I have included some of my own family history to put this into context.

I believe that trauma is usually at the root of psychological distress and I hope these stories illustrate that. Each one demonstrates how our early history affects us for the rest of our lives, influencing the ways in which we relate to the world and to other people, according to how our main carers related to us as we were growing up. This is the basis of John Bowlby's Attachment Theory (Bowlby, 1997); I hope the following stories prove how prescient he was in understanding that the adult we each become is mainly due to the way we were looked after, understood and cared for – or not, as the case may be – when we were young. Wordsworth summed it up succinctly even earlier in his *Intimations of Immortality* by the single line "The child is father to the man".

Storytelling is very much part of therapy and I have always enjoyed listening to stories and telling them as well. Many of those I have heard during my work have been painful and traumatic but that is part of the job. The ones I have chosen to tell are not necessarily the most extreme, but I hope they will show the healing power of relating them. Along the way I have made many mistakes, as all people do, so not all of these stories have a successful ending. However, I have included them to illustrate the process and how things can sometimes go wrong.

The stories contained in the book are as follows:

**Chapter 1: Who am I?**
The first chapter describes the reasons why I became a psychotherapist and tells the story of one of my earlier clients who turned out to be suffering from Dissociative Identity Disorder (DID). The therapy was twice a week for three years and then once a week for a further six months.

**Chapter 2: Loss and love**
I continue with my personal story and then describe a therapy with a woman who came to me because she felt she had not bonded with her six-year old daughter who had terrible temper tantrums, caused havoc in the house and was intensely jealous of her six-month old brother. The therapy only lasted for four sessions, much to my surprise as I thought it would take much longer, but it worked. When I approached her for permission to use our work, she confirmed that things were still going well.

**Chapter 3: "You're not helping me, this is a waste of time, I don't know why I keep coming"**
This chapter continues my story and then details a three-and-a-half year therapy with a justifiably angry woman who constantly tried to sabotage the work. She had been in therapy many times before and saw this as "the last chance saloon" and eventually left, having worked through a lot of problems and feeling more at peace with herself.

**Chapter 4: Reclaiming love**
After some more of my own history, this chapter tells the story of a therapy with a man in his 30s who came to see me after an

unsuccessful course of cognitive behavioural therapy (CBT), because of his depression, an extremely poor relationship with his mother and issues regarding his sexuality. The therapy lasted for over three years and finished with him saying he had "reclaimed his mother". He also felt more at ease with his sexuality and was no longer depressed.

## Chapter 5: Therapy with an elderly couple
Here I tell the story of a therapy with an 84-year old man, in his own home, as he had suffered a stroke and was confined to a wheelchair. His family requested therapy because he had become almost mute after his 21-year old grandson committed suicide and he could not accept it. His wife requested to sit in on the therapy so it was a most unusual one. I saw them for about 20 months, at the end of which he was talking more to his family and had taken on board the fact that his grandson had intended to kill himself. It is a sad story but one that I feel needed to be shared.

## Chapter 6: "I'm someone with a future and not just a past"
This is mainly concerned with a three-and-a-half year therapy with a woman in her 40s who had been brought up in care and was angry, depressed and weary of life. Her transformation, through being able to tell her story and have it witnessed and validated, was quite remarkable.

## Chapter 7: Baking the cake
Chapter 7 explores the background environment of three very different people who came for therapy, examining how the "ingredients" in their upbringings formed their identities and led them to their particular problems. The first example is Veronica who came from a complicated family, whose father was married three times and her mother five times, and how she, as the third child in a family of four, became someone with a desperate need to control her immediate environment, having had no control of it when she was young. The second example is Rick, an only child born to only children, who became a shy and lonely person with

obsessive compulsive disorder (OCD) tendencies and difficulties in sustaining relationships. He reluctantly came for therapy at the insistence of his mother after two failed marriages and a further three failed relationships, plus the possibility of losing contact with his three children. The third example is Catherine, the younger sister of a very successful man who was always "the blue-eyed boy" in the family, and the struggles she had to maintain a feeling of self-worth in her marriage and as a mother.

## Chapter 8: Granite man
This chapter is about a therapy with a man who came from an ostensibly loving family and yet suffered from unwitting emotional neglect and deprivation by not having his essential emotional needs met in childhood. Despite exploring in detail the many factors causing his difficulties – such as chronic shyness, depression, relationship problems and deep feelings of regret, guilt and anger – his "dismissive" attachment style meant that ultimately he could not proceed with the therapy when it became too close to home, and so his problems remained unresolved. However, I hope he learnt useful things from the therapy.

## Chapter 9: Shadow woman
Chapter 9 is about a woman, again from an ostensibly loving family, whose many difficulties arose from never being allowed to be herself. It took a number of years of therapy before she could emerge from the shadows.

## Chapter 10: Conclusions
This short chapter concludes my own story and presents some final thoughts based on the case examples in the book.

# Chapter 1

# Who am I?

After my mother died, my father and sister were left to live together. My father was 85, frail in body but sound in mind. My sister, Frances, was 56, sound in body but frail in mind. Sadly she was suffering from early-onset Alzheimer's. She had not yet been formally diagnosed but I knew, after accompanying her on regular six-monthly visits to The National Hospital for Neurology in Queen's Square, what she was suffering from. I had witnessed her struggle with the memory tests she was given and could see the deterioration at every visit. Between them, she and Dad more or less made one complete person.

For nearly a year I managed both households, taking both my father and sister to their various health appointments, shopping for and with my father, helping my sister as she was gradually eroding from within. One Tuesday evening my father rang us almost in tears and said that Frances had flooded their bathroom, again, and could we please help. My husband and I drove over and cleaned up, and on the way home he said to me, "They can't go on like this." "I know," I said, "but what more can we do than we are already doing?" He paused and then said, "They'll have to come and live with us." I looked at him. "Do you know what you're saying?" I said. "Yes," he said. "I've been thinking about it. Obviously they can't literally come and live with us – there just isn't the room – but if we sold our house and their flat we could buy somewhere where we can all live together." I was stunned and tears came into my eyes as I wondered how many husbands would even think to suggest such a thing.

Back at home we asked our sons to join us for a family chat. They were then aged 18 and 16 and we sat around discussing the situation and its ramifications. All of us had a fairly clear idea of what lay ahead. After about an hour, while we thrashed out the logistics and whether or not we could realistically take this on, our elder son got up and said, "Well, it's going to be hell but we have to do it." That about summed up the situation and he was right.

That weekend we put it to Dad and Frances and Dad was only too relieved to relinquish the terrible burden that had been foisted on him. Frances, however, was not willing. They had lived in their flat for 39 years and she was still compos mentis enough to know that a change of scene would be very difficult for her, apart from the fact that she liked where they lived and was familiar with the area. Sadly, she had no real choice in the matter as we all knew that it was becoming increasingly difficult for Dad to manage, especially as they lived in a first floor flat where there was no lift and his arthritis was making walking very difficult. It was this aspect that finally persuaded Frances as she understood that Dad would probably not be able to manage the stairs for much longer.

We then set about the task of finding a new place to live. Our elder son was at university and our younger was taking his "A" levels, so I concentrated on the house search with my husband. We saw about four houses for each one that we took Dad and Frances to visit and my Dad vetoed all of them very quickly. Eventually my husband saw an advertisement for some new houses being built, just 14 of them, very near to where his brother lived, so we went to have a look. We looked round the show house, which of course looked beautiful, but I could see from the plans that the most suitable one for our needs had not yet been built. There was only one design like it. We took Dad and Frances to see the show house, which my Dad loved as it was so spacious and clean and inviting-looking. We decided we would take the one that was in the process of being built. We then had to sell both of our places which all took around one year to achieve.

We finally all moved in. Our house sale was completed two weeks before their flat sale so we had time in which to get things in order before they arrived. Our elder son had not even seen the house before he came home for his first vacation from university. Our new home had four bedrooms but he did not want to share a room with his brother, something they had done throughout their childhood, so we bought him a sofa bed which was placed in the downstairs living room and that was where he slept on his visits home.

How we managed to live together would take up a whole book on its own and is not really the subject of this one, so I shall just say that it took a good while for everyone to adjust and adapt. My biggest problem was never having any time on my own and I began to realise how much I relished that space in which I could just "be". I could not just "be" for the next three-and-a-half years. However, during that period I had little bursts of time; preparing vegetables in the kitchen, having a shower, ironing, when I could be alone with my thoughts for a while. Those thoughts gradually led me to become aware of the many reasons why and how my only sister had developed early-onset Alzheimer's. I thought back over her life and how badly damaged she already was years before I was born.

Her father had died when she was only three months old, during World War II, leaving our mother a young widow with a tiny baby. Mum went back to live with her mother who looked after Frances while Mum went back to work full-time. Our grandfather was her surrogate father but he died when Frances was three. Already there were huge traumas in Frances's life; loss of her father and later her grandfather, awareness of our mother's sadness, grief and despair, change of environment and adapting to other people caring for her. Then when Frances was three, it was decided that children living in London should be evacuated to the country to save them from the danger and stress of the bombings. Frances was one of those evacuated, on her own as our mother had to continue working to provide for the family. A childless couple on a farm in Wales took her in and looked after her for the duration of the war. I can only imagine the sense of loss and abandonment she must have felt. I believe her trust in people was shattered by the time she was five. Aged five she came home again, however, our mother had to continue working full-time, and she decided that the best way to care for Frances and enable her to mix with children of her own age, was to send her to boarding school. Frances told me later that she hated boarding school and cried a great deal and that the headmistress used to take her into her own room and let her play on the floor until she had "settled down". Our mother met my father during the time Frances was at boarding school. They married when Frances was six-and-a-half and eventually she came home to a "normal" family life after I was born, when she was nearly eight.

These thoughts led me on to think about my own childhood experiences and the realisation that no one ever thought to tell me that Frances and I were in fact half-sisters. This I found out when I was 14 and it came as a huge shock to me. At the time Frances was living in Israel so we had no chance to talk about it. Obviously she knew because she was old enough to remember when my parents married. Much later she told me that she had been told never to say anything about it to me and she never did. In fact, it was something I could not talk to anyone about because it clearly upset my mother – something I quickly established on the day she told me, after she had no other option when I questioned her directly. I knew I could not talk to my father about it either, as he had been in the impossible position of trying to fill the shoes of a man idealised by the rest of the family through his early death. I believe that most of my 22 first cousins also knew the situation but had been instructed not to talk to me about it. For some reason it was a family secret, one that everyone else knew about but I did not. It did explain many things of course and I now knew why Frances had green eyes when both of my parents had brown eyes. It also explained why my father was never physically demonstrative towards her, maybe thinking that might be misconstrued. He did his best to be a dutiful father to her and she loved him but she could never receive that love back, at least not unconditionally.

Around the time of us all living together I began to read a lot about psychological issues, initially in an attempt to try and understand more about Frances. When I first read about John Bowlby's Attachment Theory (Bowlby, 1997) it was like a series of fireworks going off in my head. "Yes, yes, yes," I said to myself as everything he wrote made perfect sense. I knew I had to pursue this course. There was little I could do to help Frances beyond be there for her, fight for her and protect her as much as I could and let her know that she was loved and cherished, whatever happened. However, I now felt that perhaps I could help other people. This experience, together with other life experiences, is what led me to train to become an attachment-based psychoanalytic psychotherapist.

When we moved to our new house I had been working as a doctor's receptionist, after years of being a secretary/PA before marriage. I managed to find a part-time job at a local doctor's surgery. I knew I had to keep on working to save my sanity if nothing else. This particular job allowed me to see the disconnection between people with health problems and the doctors who treat them. There was such a split between physical health and mental/psychological health – whereas I knew that the two were inextricably linked – and it was a complete puzzle to me as to why doctors did not address this. The mind/body connection is fundamental and yet is so often completely over-looked or ignored in traditional western medicine, although this is now changing.

Once I had applied to train and had passed the necessary interviews, I needed to start on my own personal therapy. This was something I had never experienced in any depth before, although most of the other members of my training group had been in therapy, some of them for years. I was required to have at least one year of therapy before being allowed to start the course. I was assigned a therapist and so the work began. It was invaluable to me at the time as I was able to offload all my anxieties, fears, sadness, grief, anger and despair at what was happening to Frances. Many of my sessions were spent in talking through my feelings around Frances. It also gave me time and space to explore my own background and what had led me to where I was at that moment. The therapy continued throughout the four-year training and for a further two years afterwards. I do not really understand how some people can become counsellors or therapists without having had therapy of their own. How can they help to resolve other people's issues if they have not yet dealt with the very same issues within themselves? This might go some way to explain why some people find they are not helped by therapy, as I suspect they have seen therapists who have not explored their own childhood experiences with the help of an empathic therapist.

Of course, it was not just my experience of looking after Dad and Frances that led me down the psychotherapy route. Psychology had long been an interest of mine and I had been reading books on the subject for many years. During my adolescence, things became quite rocky and I did see a psychiatrist at one point in my life, but it was on the NHS and consisted of a one-hour session every six weeks or so. Luckily I saw a wonderful psychiatrist, a young Australian who was open to new ideas. He was the one who initially started me on my long journey into psychotherapy.

During the four years of training, we read many books and articles and gradually began to know the main people involved in the psychotherapeutic world, a world just as power-crazy and driven as any other. The fallings-out and verbal wars between the different factions was a revelation and just proved that we are all human; however learned and wise we are in our own particular field, we can fall prey to petty jealousy and overpowering envy. Learning to negotiate this world within the small organisation with which I trained was the biggest eye-opener. Even in our training group of ten people there were divisions and factions and power struggles. I have remained in touch with five of those from our group and we meet up at regular intervals.

After two years we began to see clients under the care of our supervisors. My very first training client introduced me to a path I have been exploring ever since. She spent our first session talking about her childhood which had been a particularly traumatising one. As we walked downstairs at the end of the session, she said to me, "Can you explain something to me? Sometimes I am a boy. I don't mean I feel like a boy. I actually *am* a boy – sometimes. What does that mean?" I hesitated and said, "Well, I'm not entirely sure but we can talk this through properly when I see you again next week." As soon as she had gone, I rang my supervisor to tell her what had just happened and we then discussed it at our weekly meeting. My very first client turned out to be suffering from Dissociative Identity Disorder (DID), a relatively rare condition which some psychiatrists question to this day even though it is officially recognised. However, I have seen a number of clients suffering from this disorder. Some knew they had DID whilst others did not and the true nature of their problem only gradually became apparent after they had been seeing me for a while.

# Paul

One of these, a man I will call Paul, came to see me after he had seen an NHS counsellor for eight sessions. He was a train driver and, sadly, a woman had committed suicide by jumping in front of his train. This had left him with Post Traumatic Stress Disorder (PTSD) and his company put him on sick leave for six months and arranged for him to see a counsellor. After the eight sessions, which included a treatment known as Eye Movement Desensitization and Reprocessing (EMDR – see Note 1) that he found re-traumatizing, she recommended he continue with psychotherapy as she could tell that he needed much more work. That is how he came to see me.

Paul arrived for his first session looking nervous. He was a man of about 6' 4", strongly built, shaven headed and heavily but beautifully tattooed. He told me he was married with three young children but his marriage was extremely volatile for all kinds of reasons. He was also still mourning the loss of his oldest sister who had died 18 months earlier from cancer. His parents had divorced when he was 21 and he remembered their marriage as being difficult, punctuated by periods of drunken rages and violence on the part of his father. He said he was terrified of his father throughout his childhood as his older brother was his father's favourite and somehow whatever he did seemed to anger his father. He reflected that maybe he reminded his father of himself when he was young. He had vivid memories of being in bed as a child with his parents downstairs when suddenly he would hear his father's footsteps on the stairs running up and he knew that his mother had related some misdeed of his and his father was coming up to punish him. His father was usually drunk by this time and would beat him mercilessly and Paul would lie in bed afterwards shaking and crying. He knew he could not turn to his mother for any comfort or reassurance. He said that even if she had just stroked his head it would have helped but she never did. Even now as a man in his late 30s some minor trigger could catapult him back to that small terrified child.

Paul was worried that he would not have enough time with me to sort out his many problems; however he was coming twice a week for a minimum of two years, a requirement of the scheme he was on whereby he could have therapy at a discounted rate. During the first three months I heard a great deal about his childhood and the relationship he had with his wife – who was anorexic, drank to excess and would take drugs if she could get hold of them. She had taken an overdose a year before he started to see me and he had thought she would not pull through. He had sat in the hospital corridor rehearsing how he could tell his children that their mother had died. She did pull through but it had a very damaging effect on his children, particularly the youngest who was six. She did not want to go to school and leave her mother, so every morning was a battle with Paul reassuring her that things would be all right. Often the children would find their mother drunk and would call him as they could not wake her up. Consequently, his home life was stressful and chaotic, and Paul did more than his fair share of cooking, cleaning, washing and ironing. He could not bear the thought of his children lacking clean clothes to wear or not having a proper cooked meal each evening. In many ways it was as though he had four children to care for instead of three. At times his wife, instead of supporting him, needed even more support than the children. He loved his children dearly and he also loved his wife, but their lifestyle caused him unimaginable stress.

During those first three months of therapy I sometimes felt confused, as Paul would often not remember what we had discussed in a previous session even though it had been a few short days ago. He also complained of sometimes losing time, once forgetting a whole 12 hour period which was unaccounted for in his mind. He told me that sometimes, when he and his wife were out, he encountered people who seemed to know him but he had no recollection of ever meeting them. One day he told me about finding papers in the waste bin, which turned out to be some poems he had written. He read them and knew he must have written them but had no recollection of doing so. At that moment all these things slotted into place and I asked him if he ever felt he was someone else. There was a long silence and then he said, "Yes. I often find I am someone else." I asked him if he could describe who he might be at different times. He started to tell me about the other inhabitants of his world, people he had never mentioned to anyone else in case they thought he was crazy. Paul was an excellent artist and had shown me drawings he had done of his children. They were of the highest standard and yet he said there were times when he could barely hold a pencil properly, let alone know how to use one to draw or shade. It was as though at times he was someone who could not draw at all. Everything seemed to add up and I told him a bit about Dissociative Identity Disorder (DID), which he had never heard of before. The reality is that people who suffer from DID are usually the victims of a crime – a crime that they suffer from for the rest of their lives while its perpetrators rarely have to face up to what they did. The consequences are nearly always borne by their victims.

Paul asked me what I thought of him and how I viewed him. I said that I could see a tall, well-built man but that I could also sense the scared little boy inside him. He sat back and gave a deep sigh and relaxed into the cushions. "I'm so glad you said that," he said. "For so many years I refused to see that little boy and I didn't think anyone else could see him either, or I wouldn't let them see him. As a teenager I could be a right bastard, always getting into trouble and fights, usually not of my making, but trouble seemed to follow me around." He spoke of when he had potentially put himself in danger in the street by intervening in a threatening situation where another man had a knife, which he could have used on him. He asked me why he did that and I said I thought it was his way of compensating for not being able to defend himself when he was younger and therefore wanting to defend the underdog once he was an adult. I also felt that harked back to his childhood imaginary friend Zero, whom he had invented as a superhero, who could overcome all enemies. He nodded and asked how we were going to tackle the vulnerable little boy inside him, who was so at odds with his actual appearance. I said I thought he should try to imagine how other people feel too and that many of those who seem confident and sure of themselves may also be feeling just as vulnerable inside. He nodded and added that he really enjoyed our sessions because he felt "free to play" and exchange thoughts and ideas.

We looked at how arguments in Paul's childhood had always meant big trouble and how he had never seen them resolved in a civilized manner, so he had never absorbed the fact that things could be worked out without resorting to violence or very bad feelings. This resonated with him and he said he felt he could keep a calmer perspective on things now. This led on to us talking about his PTSD and I said I thought the suicide had been the final straw but that he had actually been suffering from PTSD for much longer. The tragic suicide had catapulted it to pole position. He said again how guilty he felt that he had done nothing to stop it. I replied that really he had been unable to prevent it as he was driving the train when she jumped, and could never have prevented it even if he had been able to see her in advance, which of course he had not. He said that intellectually he knew that was the case, but there was some gut feeling that he could have done more. We spoke more about that and how he could not protect everyone all the time.

He said that on bright and sunny days he just wanted to forget all adult responsibilities like the mortgage and bills and run free like a child. He felt a great sense of release when he could immerse himself in childish things, yet always remembered at some point he was an adult. I said that unfortunately he did have to accept he was an adult but that he could always feel free to indulge his childish needs when playing with his own children or doing something creative like his drawing or writing poetry or making music.

Over the next few months we uncovered the other personalities who shared his life. I asked him if he could note them down for me with all their characteristics and he eventually gave me a comprehensive list. It included a young woman, a scared little boy, a guardian who kept watch on all the others, a dreamer who was the artistic one, a coping, macho man who was in control of all things and took charge when the others could not cope and, finally, a terrifying man who he referred to as "Mr No-Going Back". This was the one who scared him most, as if he ever showed himself then it meant that things were dire indeed. He only came when nothing else would work and he was the one to whom all the others would defer. He had no fear and no sense of proportion and could cause devastation. Paul said he now realised that he had spent most of his life being either Macho Man, in order to cope with day-to-day life, or the Dreamer, with occasional bouts of one of the others – although little triggers could catapult him back to the scared little boy.

By this time he had managed to find another job, which certainly did not stretch him but was a way to earn a living until such time as he felt able to take on something more responsible. He told me that as a younger man he had worked in an office, but due to his time lapses he often forgot things so would write a to-do list every day, just to remind him of the simple tasks he had to do – those which other people would have done automatically. Having a fractured mind that has split your personality into various fragments is completely exhausting.

We explored the reasons behind this fragmentation and it was apparent that he had never felt safe during his childhood, due not only to his father's violent outbursts but also his mother's volatility. He said that she had been horribly abused as a child and teenager by family members, as well as by lodgers who rented rooms in their house. Paul had also been sexually abused by a priest when he was about eight or nine. He told his mother at the time, who believed him due to her own childhood experiences, and she informed the school. There was an inquiry and he remembered being questioned by a policeman who came to the house. However, he did not remember what happened to the priest except that he no longer taught at the school. He was often picked on at school for minor misdemeanours and his sensitivity was definitely not appreciated, either by his father or his peers, so he kept it well hidden. He had all the ingredients in his childhood to make multiplicity possible, as it is a creative response to intolerable and frightening situations that a child cannot do anything about. The only way he had of coping with the terrors of his life was to dissociate from them, disappear inside himself and create another world which seemed safer. He had done this a number of times as he was growing up which was how he had developed multiple personalities. Each of these personalities came about as a means of protecting his inner essence. However, his essence remained as Paul, the man I listened to each week, and I explained that even though he may resort at times to hiding within a different personality, he was essentially himself. Having said this, when someone is in a different personality (or alter) he (or she) may behave unlike his "essential" self until such time as he returns to his main being. Some people with DID live in their different alters much of the time, switching from one to another depending on what life is triggering them to do.

Paul continued to see me twice a week for nearly three years, during which time he began to know himself very well and to recognise the triggers that could send him into one of his other personalities. These included condensation on the inside of windows, reminding him of Sunday dinners eaten in the kitchen in silence apart from the scraping of cutlery, music playing from an upstairs window and certain smells and sounds. Eventually he was able to join up some of his other people so that they amalgamated. By the time we finished his therapy he had started another better-paid job, more commensurate with his abilities, and he had managed to reconcile his inner child with his adult self incorporating his artistic side, the Dreamer, and also Macho Man, so he had become a more well-rounded person. There was still the spectre of Mr No-Going Back but he felt he would never need to disappear into him. He fully acknowledged his feminine side – he used to refer to it as "that woman" but now accepted that it was just part of him.

We also discussed his relationships with his wife, children, siblings and friends but for the purposes of his particular story I have concentrated mainly upon his DID as it had such an impact on his life. Some people still dispute the reality of Dissociative Identity Disorder but I believe that may be because they have never really met or listened to someone who suffers from it, or possibly they have done but have been unable or unwilling to comprehend what it means for them. I have met too many people who suffer from DID to argue about its existence. It nearly always manifests itself as a result of extreme trauma in their early childhood, as the only way in which they can cope with an otherwise unbearable situation. In many ways it is even more difficult to treat people who have been severely traumatised but have found no way to protect themselves from that intolerable situation. It lives with them each and every day of their lives unless and until they are helped to understand it and process it.

I know of sufferers of DID who have confided in doctors or psychiatrists only to be told that they are delusional. To have their suffering and trauma disbelieved in such a callous way almost defies belief but that is probably because those practitioners cannot themselves believe what this person is telling them. To have one's story listened to and believed and validated is one of the healing processes of therapy and, arguably, the most important one.

## Note 1

Eye Movement Desensitization and Reprocessing (EMDR) is a psychotherapy treatment that was originally designed to alleviate the distress associated with traumatic memories.

# Chapter 2

# Loss and love

Before I became a mother I had not read many books about mothering. I decided to follow my instincts and remember the good parts from my own mother. One thing I certainly knew was that I wanted to stay at home with my children for at least the first few years of their lives. The main reason for this was because my mother had gone back to work when I was three months old. I understood that this was from necessity but nevertheless it meant that she was not around much while I was growing up. My husband and I discussed whether or not I could stay at home once we had children and, thankfully, by the time we had our firstborn it was possible, although money was tight. These days it is much harder for the majority of mothers to stay at home. I feel that successive governments do not attach enough importance to the early bonding of mothers, or other primary carers, to young children who need the security and consistency of having the same loving people around them during their earliest formative years. I did return to work, part-time, when the boys were both settled at school.

My mother had to employ a live-in nanny to look after me from the age of three months. Nanny Roberts stayed with us until I was two-and-a-half but she only really liked looking after little babies. Once they started to assert themselves and she could not have complete control of them she lost interest – or did not have the energy or patience to continue. I have no memories of Nanny Roberts although my mother told me some stories of how they had clashed over my upbringing, and Frances told me she found her a bit scary. I assume she must have given me consistent and secure care and I do not know how I reacted once she left.

The story of how my mother came to employ Nanny Roberts is interesting. She had placed an advertisement for a nanny and Nanny Roberts replied. However, she was working in Scotland at the time, being Scottish herself, so my mother interviewed her over the telephone. My mother was so impressed with her beautiful speaking voice and obvious experience that she hired her on the spot. My father went to meet her from the station having no idea what she looked like. My mother expected a tall, elegant woman purely from the impression she had been given from her voice. However, Nanny Roberts was very small and hunched over, probably from many years of looking after tiny babies. She was also much older than either of my parents had envisaged. Perhaps that was why she had applied for the job as it may have been difficult to find work at her age.

Nanny Roberts was accustomed to working in large households with proper nurseries and staff. It must have come as quite a shock to her to work for a Jewish family who lived in a small flat. She was more used to aristocratic Scottish families who lived in draughty country houses. Apparently, she liked being included in family mealtimes, something that she had not experienced before. She also liked Jewish food and was impressed with the quantity and quality of the food she was given. She told my mother that the households of her previous employers were usually more interested in drink rather than food. She was also unused to the interest that my parents took in their children. She normally had complete control in the nursery and just displayed the children to their parents for an hour or so before the children had their supper. She believed that those parents did not seem that interested in their children and just wanted someone to look after them until they were sent to boarding school at the age of seven or eight. I have often wondered why some people have children at all when they clearly do not want the responsibility of looking after them, but still want them to turn out as civilised human beings. I have enormous sympathy for Nick Duffell's views on boarding schools and the kind of people who emerge from them (Duffell, 2000); often stifled, emotionally constipated people who harbour a lot of repressed anger and despair and have little idea of how to relate to others – and then repeat the pattern with their own children. Unfortunately, many of these people, mostly men, finish up governing our country.

Once Nanny Roberts left us, my mother then employed a series of helps and au pair girls throughout the rest of my childhood. I started attending all-day nursery at the age of three and I certainly remember that. The school was in Devonshire Street, was run by two sisters, and the other children were mainly titled. I believe I may have been the only Miss. I had to sit an interview before being accepted – because I spoke well, due to being brought up by Nanny Roberts, I passed. I have vague memories of the school; colouring-in, playing with jigsaws, everyone being sent for an afternoon sleep, two to a bed. I remember a long staircase and the lingering smell of cooked cauliflower and going for walks in Regent's Park, holding hands with another child as we trooped off in a crocodile holding the coat tails of the child in front. I remember sitting on a rush mat listening to stories read out loud by one of the teachers. I loved the stories. At the end of the day many women dressed in brown uniforms would arrive to collect their charges. My mother came to collect me on her way home from work. We would walk to Baker Street station to get the train home to Osterley, where we lived until I was four. Often we could not get a seat on the train and my mother would hold me with one arm while strap-hanging with the other. If she was offered a seat I would sit on her lap and play with the little toy she usually brought along to keep me amused. I now realise what a hard life my mother had, working every day whilst trying to look after two children with an eight year age gap between them. No wonder I do not remember her ever playing with me, although she did occasionally read me bedtime stories. It was these memories that made me determined to stay home with my own children.

Our elder son was born in the early evening and I can clearly remember his newborn face staring at me in those first few minutes after birth. He looked at me quizzically and intently as if to say "So, here you are", and I was in awe of his amazing navy-blue eyes. I had never seen eyes that colour before and could hardly believe I had produced this wondrous baby. By the next morning his eyes were dark brown but I will never forget my newborn's navy-blue eyes and feel privileged to have seen them. I have never seen eyes of that colour since.

Not only did I know very little about babies but I also knew very little about males generally, apart from those I had worked with as an adult. Having just one sister and being brought up in a largely female household (my mother had five sisters), the only men I really knew well were my father and my relatively new husband. Our son was born one week before our third wedding anniversary – an early anniversary present. My husband was the youngest of three brothers so he equally knew little about women. Together we learned about each other and I approached the role of motherhood without many preconceptions. All I knew was that I loved my baby fiercely and unconditionally and would have done anything to keep him safe, secure and as contented as possible. With this in mind, I did not hesitate to pick him up whenever he cried as I reasoned he had to be crying for a reason – it was my job to discover what that reason was and to alleviate it as best I could. Fortunately, I had friends who also had small babies, so we pooled our knowledge and helped each other to negotiate the various pathways through our babies' sleeping habits, eating regimes and behaviour issues. We all learned from each other and found the best way to handle our own unique and individual babies. That was the problem with the books I did start to read. They seemed to take little account of the fact that each baby is an individual with its own unique responses.

When eventually I came to read John Bowlby and his Attachment Theory (1997) it just resonated completely with my own experience and made sense all round. I understood why I had developed an ambivalent/preoccupied attachment to my mother and a dismissive/avoidant one to my father. I also realised how damaged Frances had become due to all the disrupted attachments in her early childhood. I wish that Frances had been able to have therapy to help her reprocess and work through some of her own issues but she was such a private person, I am not sure she would have wanted to share her inner world with a therapist. I am also convinced that her early traumas predisposed her towards developing the dementia that eventually killed her. Why would she not wish to block off memories of her painful past? Unfortunately that "blocking off" took over her entire life. While she was being investigated at The National Hospital for her early-onset Alzheimer's, they discovered that she was suffering from an auto-immune disease, Scleroderma. That her body should turn against itself seemed almost inevitable in its logic of trying to cope with a lifetime of unexplored and repressed pain. Maybe if doctors and researchers explored more into people's backgrounds and early life experiences, instead of concentrating purely on the physiological, then perhaps some answers might emerge as to why some people develop dementia and many other diseases while others do not. Maybe it might even be possible to stop the inevitable deterioration if people were offered therapy as a way of helping them to release their painful memories and have them witnessed and validated and then re-processed, instead of them invading the brain and causing massive disruption and eventual erosion.

If people who have been traumatized in early life are given the opportunity to work through their feelings with someone who cares about their wellbeing and who can help them to feel safer within themselves, then it is possible that further damage can be avoided. If a parent realises that something has gone wrong in the early years and is willing to change things while the child is still young, then there is every hope that there will be no long-lasting permanent damage. One such parent was Irina.

# Irina

Irina came to see me because she was worried about the behaviour of her six-year old daughter. Irina was born in Russia to a poor family. She was 37 when she came to see me and it was the first time she had tried therapy. Her father was a drunkard and they never had much of a relationship. When drunk he was violent and she had witnessed her mother being beaten up on many occasions. Her parents divorced when she was 14 and she had little contact with her father after that. She had a sister five years older than her but she was not close to her; her sister was her mother's favourite and Irina always felt left out and the outsider.

Irina developed a very close relationship when she was 15 with a school friend, Olga, and they were best friends for ten years. She said that some people may even have thought their relationship was a sexual one, as they were so close, but she said it was "a pure friendship". When they were 25, Olga complained that Irina had changed and preferred other things and she put an end to their friendship. Irina was devastated and cried over this broken friendship for months afterwards. She said she had never got over it as she had only ever felt love towards Olga. She could not understand why Olga did not feel the same way towards her any longer. We discussed how this might have affected her and she said she had remained friendly with Olga's mother who had taken Irina under her wing.

When Irina was 18, her mother was ill with cancer and the hospital eventually told her there was nothing more they could do for her – so they sent her home to die. Irina looked after her until her death even though she was not close to her. Two years later her father died from alcoholism. When she was 28 her older sister also died, from a drug overdose, as she had developed a drug habit while at university. At the time Irina was working as a waitress and one of her customers was an Englishman, 20 years older than her, who used to frequent the restaurant where she worked. He asked her out one day and they developed a relationship. He was working in Russia but after he went back to England, he returned to visit her six times and asked her to marry him and come to England with him. Although this was rather a scary prospect, she had fallen in love with this man and had nothing to keep her in Russia, so she followed him to England and they married. He had been married before and had a 20-year old daughter with whom he had a difficult relationship.

Soon after their marriage Irina became pregnant and had their first child, Nadia. Nadia's birth was very traumatic. Irina had a totally unsympathetic female doctor and she noticed the nurses all seemed to shrink into themselves when this doctor came in the room. They took her to theatre to do an emergency Caesarean, as the baby's heart rate had dropped, but she gave birth before this could happen. The doctor stitched her up afterwards without anaesthetic and told her to stop screaming as she was no longer in labour. The doctors looked at Nadia and were talking about a "syndrome"; when she asked what syndrome, they said they thought Nadia had Down's Syndrome. Irina said it was as though someone had chopped part of her away and although she loved her baby, she felt totally disconnected from her and could not look at her. It was as though a shutter had come down between them. When they took Nadia home they both wondered about this diagnosis, as she looked ordinary to them, and neither her husband nor Irina could see any evidence of Down's Syndrome. The hospital had given them leaflets about it, but no one had talked to them. Three weeks later the hospital carried out tests on Nadia and declared that she did not have Down's Syndrome after all. No one apologised for their initial error and it left Irina wondering for the first year of Nadia's life. She said she could not look into Nadia's eyes and although she did everything for her, she knew they had not bonded. It was primarily due to her difficult relationship with Nadia that she was now seeking therapy, particularly since she had had another baby, a boy Andrei, now six months old. Nadia was extremely jealous of Andrei and had terrible temper tantrums.

Irina had begun to read about attachment and realised that she had not bonded with Nadia, and had been unable to look into her eyes for at least the first year. She now understood this even more as she had no trouble bonding with Andrei and could look at him adoringly, which she knew did not happen with Irina. Andrei suffered from eczema and we discussed the possibility of this being psychosomatic, as he could well have been picking up the tension in the house since she said it was not a happy home. She knew that Nadia was not a happy child and she really wanted to try to change things.

We talked about ways in which Irina could start to make changes. I reassured her that she could do a huge amount of reparative work – it was not too late as Nadia was still so young. She became upset and said she had read that by the time a child is five things are set. I replied that nothing is set in stone and that Nadia's brain still had enough plasticity to re-wire neural pathways in a better way. In fact, even adults' brains' neural pathways can be changed. I mentioned "love-bombing" (James, 2012) and how Nadia needed to feel that she was safe in the world – showing her how much her parents loved her and cared about her was the best thing Irina could do. We spoke of how Nadia's defiance and "naughty" behaviour could well be ways she had adopted to gain some attention from her mother. She told me of various incidents where Nadia's behaviour had been particularly trying and how she had dealt with it. Nadia often refused food and was very skinny, but then wanted to eat chocolate and screamed until she got her way. We discussed boundaries and setting up a star chart and rewards for good behaviour, instead of constant admonishment for "bad" behaviour. I suggested she might like to include Nadia in the choices and preparation of food so that she felt more involved and a bit more in control, as she was trying to exert control in other ways. I also encouraged Irina to ask Nadia more about how she was feeling as Nadia was actually very bright for her age and articulated her feelings well. She had told Irina that she did not want to live in their house and would rather live in another house with a different Mummy and Daddy. Irina said that as a child she had never felt loved by her own mother and it really upset her that Nadia now felt the way she had felt as a child. It was evidently a repeating pattern.

In our second session, Irina said that sometimes when dealing with Nadia she found herself in a helpless situation, e.g. she calls Nadia for breakfast but she does not answer. Irina calls upstairs again, but still no reply, so eventually she has to go upstairs to find her and Nadia is hiding somewhere, playing hide and seek. She found it very inconvenient to do that in the morning, when she was trying to get everyone ready in time. She had explained to Nadia that she could play hide and seek in the afternoon after getting home and Irina could then join in, but not first thing in the morning; however, Nadia was very obstinate. I said it sounded like again Nadia was trying to gain her mother's attention. She said that in the past they both used to shout at Nadia when she did not respond after two or three times but they had stopped doing this since Nadia screamed back at them, "You always shout at me"; she realised that she usually did and it was not a good thing.

She said that when Andrei was a few weeks old they were all in the car together and drove past a river and Nadia said, "Some parents throw their babies in the river". Irina found this remark very shocking and wondered where she had got that from but I said that she was being totally honest and telling them that she felt jealous of the new baby and wished he was not there. This was actually a perfectly normal reaction from a little girl who has had her parents to herself for five years and then been "pushed aside" as she might have seen it. I urged Irina to do as much as possible to reassure Nadia how much she was loved; to cuddle her, caress her and praise her whenever she did good things – rather than tell her off when she did "naughty" things – so that she was positively rewarding her for good behaviour rather than punishing her for bad behaviour. I hoped that by doing this Nadia would prefer to do the good things that elicited positive comments from her parents and would still receive the attention she craved. I also urged Irina to include her in helping to look after Andrei as she was his big sister, after all. Irina commented that she did not want to turn her daughter into a "little mother" as she was entitled to be a child herself. I agreed with her but said that it was still a fact that she was a big sister too and could feel positive about that relationship rather than harbouring feelings of jealousy. She said that generally Nadia did seem to like the baby now and often made faces at him to make him laugh. He followed her round with his eyes all the time and she often gave him toys to play with. I said that all sounded good and positive and should be encouraged. She thought that at the same time Nadia could see how much she cuddled Andrei and looked at him adoringly. She felt so guilty that she never did that with Nadia and wondered if this would leave deep scars that could never heal. I said that she would not consciously remember those times but may well have developed an ambivalent attachment style, as Irina believed that she was not consistent in the way she looked after her. However, she could now do the reparative work to ensure that Nadia did feel safe and secure within the family, and that both her parents cared about her as much as they obviously cared about Andrei. I suggested that she could set aside some specific time to be alone with Nadia and to tell Nadia that this was "her time". During this special time, she was allowed to do whatever she liked (within reason) and Irina would join her and help her in whatever games she wanted to play or stories she wanted to hear, or drawing or skipping or anything she really wanted to do, and that this was a time for them to be together. Irina said she had never really done that, although she had played with Nadia, but the play had not been led by Nadia. I said if she could do this with Nadia at least once a week, so that she would know that her mother truly cared about her, it might be very helpful.

We also discussed how Irina had developed an avoidant/

dismissive attachment style to her own mother. She recalled emailing her cousin to ask if she remembered how her mother had treated her as a child – was her older sister really the favourite or was that just in Irina's imagination? Her cousin replied that her mother had indeed preferred her older sister and had made that preference known. Irina went on to say she remembered being ridiculed by her mother for having strong feelings about things; they were not tolerated, so as a teenager she became very sarcastic instead and was not very nice at that time.

The following week she said she had been talking more to Nadia and explaining to her that she was trying to do things differently. However, Nadia did not seem to be listening much and Irina felt that her daughter did not really trust her. I said that she could continue to build up trust by showing Nadia that she was truly there for her, holding her and listening to her attentively. She said she had started to be more tactile and Nadia was responding well to that and seemed to be calmer. Irina said she had noticed that when she became agitated then that feeling was transmitted to Nadia. On the other hand, when she was relaxed then everything seemed to go more easily, so it was all down to her really, and I agreed with that. She also said that spending more time exclusively with Nadia seemed to have calmed down her temper tantrums.

Irina told me that in the past she had friends who she had just cut off if they said or did something to upset her. Having read about attachment theory, she now realised that she had an avoidant attachment style and would rather withdraw and 'lick her wounds' than confront someone or go through a period of reconciliation. She said that when she was first with her husband, she sometimes used to walk out in a huff or not speak to him for a long time. He was always patient and kind and waited until she felt better, so she gradually learnt to trust him and she said she no longer responded this way. I commented that she needed to be patient with Nadia in the same way so that she would learn to trust her mother. I felt sure that would eventually happen, particularly as Nadia was so young and Irina had taken appropriate steps to address the situation.

She said she sometimes felt as if she was frozen inside and I said that was a good description and hopefully therapy would help her to thaw out and to begin really feeling again. She said she did not want Nadia to become frozen, as she had, and I said that she was doing everything to prevent that and make things better for both of them.

Irina arrived on time for her fourth session, looking very happy and relaxed. I asked how things had been and she said, "Really good. I'm feeling fine. Nadia is much happier and so am I – and so is the whole family and I want to thank you very much." She said that her husband had commented to her that whatever her therapist had been telling her to do was working, because Nadia had changed for the better over the last couple of weeks and he was glad to see such an improvement in her. Irina said that one day Nadia had been upset and told her that she was feeling left out, so Irina asked her if she would like a hug and Nadia said "yes" and climbed onto her lap. Afterwards she skipped off and said she felt better and later told Irina that she loved her. This brought Irina close to tears as it was the first time she had ever said that. We discussed how she could continue to show Nadia how much she loves her, and to be as tactile as possible with lots of cuddles and kisses. I asked if her husband was tactile with Nadia and she said that he would show he was pleased, by saying something like "well done" but he was not physically demonstrative.

At the end of this session Irina said they were going on a family holiday. She felt that things were going so well, she did not think she needed to come and see me again. I said that was fine but if she ever did want to see me then she should get in touch. That was the last time she came.

When Irina first came to see me, I thought she would be in therapy for quite some time. In the event I was wrong about that. I think it was partly because Irina was so invested in making their relationship work that she put her heart and soul into repairing things. And also Nadia was still so young that she was able to internalise the change in her mother's behaviour. Lastly, their already strong attachment, however dysfunctional it may have felt to Irina, smoothed the way to repair their relationship much more quickly than either of us had thought possible.

I believe that for Irina to be able to tell her own story was really important, as no one had ever heard it before and she had not really understood the impact her life had had on her so far. She had been surprised when I pointed out all the losses she had suffered, because she had not really thought about them before. I explained that her husband had doubtless given her a great deal of "earned security" during the time they had known each other and this had been of tremendous help to Irina, allowing her to understand what Nadia had been missing for the first six years of her life. I hope that Irina was able to maintain a loving relationship with Nadia and that Nadia has developed into a happy and secure child.

# Chapter 3

## "You're not helping me, this is a waste of time, I don't know why I keep coming"

I remember missing my mother when I came home from school, and wishing she could be there. Friends were not invited home for tea as my mother felt it was too much of a responsibility for whichever au pair was with us at the time. However, I was occasionally invited to other children's houses and would feel wistful, if not downright envious, when their mothers collected us both from school; and the mothers would be asking their children about their day. By the time my parents came home from work, I was usually in bed; although they would come and kiss me goodnight there was not much time for chatting or going over the events of the day. Sometimes my father would read to me while my mother made dinner, or sometimes my mother would read to me if they had gone out to eat before coming home. If they arrived home too late then Frances might read me a bedtime story, or make one up. Frances invented an ongoing story about two sisters, Pinky and Rosamund, and I would often ask her for another story in their never-ending saga.

Once I learned to read, I would sit in bed reading until my parents came home; my greatest pleasure and solace was reading. Frances used to take me to the local library each week and I would take out three books and return them the following week. Among my favourites were E Nesbit, Noel Streatfield, PL Travers and Philippa Pearce and anything to do with time travel. The thought of time travel intrigued me and when I met my husband I was delighted that he too loved anything to do with time travel. Although we had fairly different tastes in books generally, this was one thing we shared. Having read extensively throughout my life, I can categorically state that fact is indeed stranger than fiction. Some of the true life stories I have heard over the years could never have been dreamed up by even the most fertile of imaginations. Make-believe pales compared to the real thing.

Relationships, self-esteem and deep-seated feelings of despair, anger or resentment are the bread and butter of therapeutic work. Many people I have worked with have suffered abuse at the hands of their parents; physical, sexual and/or emotional, and this has left them badly damaged for life. Some do not appear to have a sense of self and need to do a lot of work to reconnect with themselves. Others have lost all faith and trust in people due to having had their trust shattered when they were children. Others are so consumed by rage that they cannot feel benevolent towards anyone or anything. Allowing them to tell their personal narrative is invariably the first step towards healing their inner pain and distress. This can take a long time though and some people give up because the process becomes too painful.

# Claire

One of the first people I worked with was a woman in her late 50s who had been in therapy before, many times, but had never made peace with herself or found what she was looking for. She constantly tried to sabotage the work, criticised and disagreed with me and had terrible outbursts of rage. She complained that I did not understand her at all and that she could not get through to me. One day she said: "You're not helping me, this is a waste of time, I don't know why I keep coming." Yet she did keep coming.

Claire and I worked together for three-and-a-half years and

ultimately she left in a much happier frame of mind, hopeful about the future, having left her debilitating depression behind her. It was a "rollercoaster" therapy for me as I was constantly on the receiving end of a barrage of fury and even hate, and often felt that I was indeed wasting my time – and hers. However, we both learnt a great deal and after our time together we emerged as different people, like chrysalises from the cocoon of our intense and strained relationship.

Rachel Cusk (2002) said, "Mothers are the countries we come from" and I would expand on that by adding that they create a landscape with which we become so familiar, that we are forever after trying to recreate it or trying to escape from it. Claire's mother created a landscape so bleak, so cold, so devoid of human touch or warmth, that Claire never knew what it was like to receive unconditional love or even unconditional regard.

Claire had been seeking help for her long-term depression and relationship problems for nearly 30 years and I followed a long line of therapists and counsellors, self-help groups and self-help books that Claire had turned to over the years. She had been hospitalized for six weeks in her early 20s for depression. That was the first time she had had the opportunity to talk about her feelings and the experiences that had brought her to her depressed state.

During the course of Claire's therapy four main themes emerged, the dominant one being her feelings of anger and resentment that had simmered under the surface for so many years but gradually came out, sometimes quite explosively, during our sessions. Being allowed to voice the anger and resentment she had kept locked inside herself for so long, and finding I was able to withstand it and did not crumble under the onslaught, eventually began to let Claire heal from the hurt that had overwhelmed so much of her life.

A second theme that emerged was Claire's feelings of almost constant conflict and ambivalence. She desperately wanted attachment but a part of her always felt that any attachment would never be good enough or would be too intrusive. So she was doomed to being misunderstood, never listened to, or suffocated beneath someone else's stronger personality. She was always looking for the longed-for mother she never had and seeking a perfect attunement. Her relationships were characterized by constant ruptures which usually led to the relationship failing. These failed relationships led to frustration and disappointment and the feeling that she just could not sustain friendships and did not know how to do it. She felt that somehow there was a secret to maintaining and keeping friends that other people had but she had never been let in on. Her life was littered with the remnants of broken relationships which emphasised her feelings of abandonment and failure.

A third theme was her feeling of being crowded out or intruded upon or never being allowed enough time or space of her own. This, coupled with a feeling of always being the outsider, led Claire to feel that she was isolated in the world with no one to whom she could turn in times of distress. She also said she was painfully shy and really struggled to talk to people, often forcing herself to engage with people when really she would have preferred to keep silent and let everyone else do the talking. When she did pluck up the courage to talk she often did not know what to say and had no enthusiasm for discussing herself, her life or anything that had happened to her. She was often puzzled by other people's willingness to talk about their everyday experiences and imbue them with excitement and interest anticipating that their audience would be as enthralled to hear about them as they were to speak. I felt that this "Catch 22" situation, in which she often found herself, reflected her earliest experiences of being abandoned to deal with her own feelings and the almost total lack of mirroring that she had received. She was not only bottle-fed from birth but usually by her mother's daily help and she never remembered being held, cuddled or kissed by her mother. She was also often left to cry in a pram put in a field out of sight and out of earshot. We discussed how the impact of this early abandonment may have contributed to her long-term depression and the feeling that she did not matter to anyone and that no one could possibly care about her anyway. We talked through how she must have felt as a tiny infant when no one came and how she might have thought she was going to die or just could not survive a moment longer. As an adult she rationalized this feeling as being one of utter hopelessness and bleakness.

The final theme was a bulimic attitude which led Claire to drink in someone else's energy or enthusiasm until she eventually felt overwhelmed or consumed by them and then had to spit it out again. She found it hard to regulate this and had in fact suffered from bulimia in her 20s for about 10 years. A previous counsellor helped her to overcome this but the bulimic attitude still prevailed. Claire also hated the feeling of dependence that she developed with me once the therapy was under way.

Claire was 57 when the therapy began. She was unmarried and lived on her own. She worked part-time as an acupuncturist. She was a petite, attractive woman with a slightly elfin look about her and she was always neatly dressed in well co-ordinated clothes but she never wore make-up and only occasionally wore jewellery. However, she had a care-worn look and usually a serious expression, rarely smiling or laughing. She had lived in London for nearly 40 years but had grown up in rural Ireland, the third of four children and the only girl in the family. Hers was not a close family. She was teased and bullied by her older brothers and she in turn teased and bullied her younger brother. There was no privacy either and her brothers could walk freely into her room and look at her things such as her diary. Her mother was largely unavailable and much of Claire's upbringing was left to a young woman, Bridie, who was her mother's help around the house and came in every day. Claire said she felt closer to her father during her childhood. Her father ran the village hardware shop and her mother helped him out while also looking after her frail mother-in-law, who lived with them. After her mother-in-law died, an elderly aunt came to live with them and she looked after her too. They had a higher standard of living than most of the other villagers and Claire felt this set her apart, so her feelings of being different and isolated started at a very early age.

Claire had been a clever girl and won a scholarship to a boarding school run by nuns. Her father took her on a trip to America to visit his family there as a reward for this, when she was 12, but it only caused jealousy and resentment among her brothers and mother, who stayed home to allow her to go. She did not enjoy the holiday. At about the same age Claire became her father's confidante and companion on walks after work. On these walks, he would talk to her about nature, art and literature and confide in her about his worries regarding her siblings; one of her brothers in particular, whom he referred to as "the quare fellow". Claire enjoyed these walks, especially the time with her father, and developed a love of nature and of cycling around the countryside. In London cycling was one of her favourite pastimes.

Claire said she never had any close friends at school. During her first term as a boarder there was an incident with another girl which undermined her confidence in herself and made her feel she could never have the courage of her own convictions. This girl was popular with the other pupils and the nuns but Claire saw that underneath her "goody-goody" image she was in fact quite manipulative and underhand. This outraged Claire at the time and she confronted her about her "whited sepulchre" façade and tried to get some of the other girls, who knew what she was really like, to back her up. Unfortunately, this girl was too charismatic and popular for Claire to stand a chance of showing her up in her true colours and eventually she backed down and "went over to the other side" as she put it. Thereafter, she never felt brave enough to confront or challenge anyone again. Claire often referred back to this incident and her inability to stand up for herself or have the courage of her own convictions.

During her first few years at school Claire was very religious. She also had a crush on one of the nuns, who later went on to become the Mother Superior. She worked hard to please this nun and did well academically but never managed to forge a close relationship with any of the girls. During school holidays she would over-eat at home and always put on weight; by the end of the holidays her uniform would no longer fit her and her mother would sigh and say, "look at the size of you," and Claire felt terrible about herself. Back at school, she would starve herself and exercise in her cubicle at night, with the curtains drawn round her while the others slept, in order to lose the weight. In her 20s, while studying nursing, she discovered how to control her weight by being sick after eating and decided this was a good way to regulate herself, and it took some years of counselling for her to overcome this.

Claire won a place at university but found she could not cope with being on her own and organizing her life. She found it all too overwhelming and failed dismally after her first year. Her parents suggested she go to London and take up nursing, as her mother had been a nurse before her marriage. So, Claire came to London and started living in a nurses' home at one of the big London teaching hospitals. Unfortunately, she did not take to nursing. Although she was able to learn the theory, she found it very hard being on a ward, could not cope with people on a one-to-one basis and resented having to do certain tasks. She said she felt like a 12-year old expected to take on adult responsibilities. We discussed how this may have come about because she was so used to being regimented at boarding school, always being told what to do and when to do it, and then finding herself in a similar environment in the nurses' home. One of the other student nurses befriended her and tried to help her. However, Claire found she spent many evenings listening to her friend's personal problems but when she tried to talk about her own problems, she found her friend not very receptive. She failed her first year exams and went back to Ireland, where she lapsed into a deep depression and eventually went into hospital for six weeks. She was given some therapy there and said this was the first time she had been allowed to talk about herself with someone who had the time to listen and who she felt might understand a little.

When Claire came out of hospital, she initially stayed with her parents, who were at a loss as to how to deal with her until, after some time not doing anything much but moping around at home, she answered an advertisement in the local paper. An elderly gentleman was looking for a housekeeper to help him run his house and care for his wife, who was an invalid after suffering a stroke. She took the position, stayed there for a year and enjoyed her time with this couple. He taught her how to cook and she helped look after his wife and generally run the household. After a year she felt much better about herself and decided to return to London. Back in London, she had a series of jobs; receptionist in a hotel, cleaning, looking after someone with Alzheimer's and secretarial work.

Whilst working as a receptionist at a hotel, one of the guests, an older divorced American, took a liking to her and invited her to go back with him to America for a holiday – for which he would pay. Without knowing very much about him, she took him up on this offer. She left her job and went to America with him for a few weeks, staying in his home. I was quite alarmed when she told me this story as I felt she had potentially put herself in considerable danger but she regarded it as an adventure. Some of the other stories she told me about experiences with men showed a recklessness that I also found worrying, as though she had very little idea of self-preservation or safety. She realised during her stay in America that he was looking for a second wife and had thought she fitted the bill but did not pressurize her when she refused. On her return to London, she found a different job and drifted from one employment to another, sometimes living in squats with friends she made along the way. She used to go to parties and various groups, where she made transitory friend-ships but often felt she was the outsider. For instance she might hear anti-Irish jokes and be very angry, but not have the courage to say anything, so would then leave and feel bad about herself. She also experimented with smoking cannabis and a few other drugs.

During this time, Claire had a series of short-term relationships with men and became pregnant during one of them. She arranged to have an abortion, even though the man did offer to help support her and the child, but not to marry her. She went for the abortion on her own, came home on her own and did not tell anyone else about it. When I asked her how she had felt at the time, she said, "I knew I couldn't look after a baby – I was just a big baby myself." Claire had started going out with boys from an early age, as her father taught her to drive when she was 16, and she used to drive herself to dances in the local villages. She went out with a number of young men and allowed them to kiss and fondle her, believing that was all they wanted from her. She never found anyone she could really talk to.

When Claire was in her early 30s she met a man, Jim, who was divorced, who really seemed to fall in love with her and they lived together for about six months. She was working for solicitors as a secretary and finding it very difficult; she would come home to Jim and be able to tell him all about her day and be listened to. She enjoyed shopping and cooking with him and became used to a certain lifestyle as he was not short of money. Early on in their relationship they went on a holiday together and she became very withdrawn and uncommunicative while they were away. She told me she could not quite believe what she was doing, going away with a man she hardly knew who was paying for her, and he became puzzled and exasperated by her. However, their relationship continued and at Christmas they went to Ireland to visit her family and stayed with one of her brothers. She had a bad cold and withdrew to their room for most of the holiday, leaving Jim to his own devices, and they broke up shortly afterwards. She was completely devastated by this and felt she had been expelled from paradise. She had to leave Jim's house and look after herself again. She said that when she was with Jim she had begun to rely on him more and more and had almost completely "lost herself". She told me that this usually happened when she became involved with a man. She used the man to offload all her problems on to, allowed him to take all responsibility for her and then became "lost". Her sense of self became totally submerged.

After her break-up with Jim she could no longer continue seeing the counsellor she had been seeing for a couple of years. Despite it being a time when she really needed to speak to someone, she broke off contact with the counsellor saying she could no longer afford to see her either in terms of money or time. She struggled for a long time to regain her equilibrium but eventually moved house and started studying for a degree again. She said this was one of the happiest times of her life although she was still battling bulimia and resorted to that when the going became rough. She had a number of transient relationships with men but nothing serious until she met an American called Roy with whom she became quite obsessed. This obsession lasted for almost ten years and seems to have totally consumed her.

Roy became the lodestone of Claire's life and she looked up to him and revered him like some kind of god. I presumed she had idealised him, as from the stories she told me about him I could not see much to like. However, Claire found his approach to life, his erudition and attitude towards people admirable. Although they did embark on a sexual relationship it was not very satisfactory. For most of the time, their relationship was a cerebral one but it appeared to have had a damaging effect on Claire, making her much more cynical, world-weary and jaded in her outlook and somehow dissolving her exuberance, vitality and joie de vivre. When she finally broke away from him she was almost sucked dry, an empty husk with nothing to sustain her. After Roy, she gave up on having intimate relationships with men. It took her about three years to recover from this peculiar attachment, during which time she relied upon various girl-friends, none of whom could provide her with the understanding and tolerance that she craved. Claire was very much a mirror-hungry personality as described by Kohut (1966 and 2009). She often said that in times of distress she would like to "go home" and be looked after, cosseted, taken care of, so she did not have to worry about anything.

At about this time her father died, having suffered from Parkinson's Disease for some years and being looked after by her mother. She felt guilty for not being there often enough to help her mother but she visited from time to time and went home for the funeral. After her father's death her mother retreated into herself and became quite reclusive. Eventually, she had to go into a care home and died shortly after that. Claire had a dread of finishing up like her mother, alone, unloved and eaten up with resentment for all the years she had spent looking after other people. This went a long way to explaining Claire's reluctance to take on any responsibilities and her unwillingness to "look after" other people, even though her job as an acupuncturist involved caring for patients. She also did driving work for a charity in the evenings.

After our first session together I felt that Claire was like someone tightly wrapped in clingfilm and part of the work in therapy was the gradual unwrapping of her. Her depression was like the tide, ever ebbing and flowing, sometimes receding and sometimes rushing in almost drowning her. She spoke of how she could never become enthusiastic about things as other people did and showed irritation when friends were obviously enjoying themselves too much, as she never could. She also despised some of her female friends who played their "femininity card" because she was so used to looking after herself and did not need a man to walk her home in the dark or put up shelves. In fact, Claire was an accomplished carpenter and had worked for a time doing this, which she enjoyed, but work was spasmodic and she did not feel secure enough in it to do it full time.

The first months of therapy were spent discovering her past and how her childhood had affected her as an adult. She clearly had a preoccupied attachment to her mother, who had never really looked after her or attuned to her in any meaningful way. She told me that at the age of nine she had cycled after her mother to try to find her when she had gone out one evening without telling Claire that she was going. She felt so abandoned, despite her father being at home, that she cycled 12 miles to her grand-mother's house where she found her mother with her sisters chatting and joking. When she arrived, tired and tearful, all her aunts laughed at her for chasing after her mother. She knew then that her mother had no idea how she felt and she told me that was when "I gave up on my mother." Her mother often used to leave the house surreptitiously to visit friends as she knew Claire would be upset at her going. This set up a feeling of suspicion and distrust in Claire from an early age. I feel she had an over-burdened self because of this lack of attunement, which explained her constant search for an all-understanding, forgiving, tolerant and calming mother figure. She had had to learn to soothe herself with no idea of how to do it and no blueprint of what it was like to have that inner core of safety and security embedded inside oneself that one could draw upon when necessary. Instead, she was just a desperately needy child over-laid with layer upon layer of covering-up, masquerading as a fully functioning adult.

During the therapy my relationship with Claire was punctuated by many disruptions and angry outbursts. She frequently accused me of not understanding her, not attuning to her, not containing her enough and of living in a different world – all reminiscent of how she had been treated by her mother. She said I waffled, missed the point, was too vague, spoke in clichés and did not use language effectively. I was also not directional enough and did not give her enough interpretations or insight. However, when I did give her interpretations she often rejected them or dismissed them with, "What good is it to know that? How does it help me now?" When I tried to provide some insights, she said I was just feeding back things she had already worked out for herself. In short, there were times when nothing I said or did was correct and I knew that whatever I could have said or done differently would have elicited the same response. Claire herself said that she was contradictory and did not know what it was that she wanted. Inside her coping, very self-sufficient, adult self there was always the angry, screaming baby crying out for attention and soothing.

After some time, I explained to Claire that, due to the lack of mirroring and attuning that had occurred in her infancy, she had never felt that sense of being held and protected, safe against all of life's vicissitudes in the knowledge that all would be well and looked after. This involved letting Claire imagine how it must feel for a baby or young child to be constantly misunderstood and never recognised or seen for herself. I used some of the examples she had given me to explain how they might have affected her at the time and how this still had an impact on her relationships today. She had had to provide herself with her own sense of inner security and therefore her sense of self was very fragile indeed, so brittle that sometimes it shattered – leaving her in a place of complete desolation and despair. This was something I had to constantly bear in mind when I felt on the painful receiving end of her many rejections and furious outbursts. At one time she said to me in a tone of weary resignation: "Well I suppose it's like everything in life – you only get what you pay for." Initially I felt totally crushed by this damning remark but at our next session I felt strong enough to challenge her and asked her how she thought I might have felt when she said that. After a couple of minutes' reflection, she said she supposed it was a hurtful thing to say and we were then able to discuss it in more detail and what it meant for her to be having therapy at a cut-price rate. The way Claire made me feel was also sometimes despairing and as though we would never get anywhere. After some sessions I felt weary, resigned and depressed and as though life had become uniformly grey and dull. I saw that this was how Claire often felt about life and its bleakness made me shudder inside.

There were a few moments of mutual recognition, however. One of them being after about 18 months of therapy when she described how she had gone out with a man for the first time in a decade. They had been to an art exhibition and out for coffee. I asked if she had dressed up for the occasion and she quickly said, "Oh no, in fact, I was wearing what I'm wearing today," which was jeans and a T-shirt. I said, "so it's almost as though you wanted to dress down, as if to say, 'This is me – take me as I am'." "Yes," she agreed and then smiled happily. "It sounds like you've done the same thing yourself."

One thing I tried to address was the way in which Claire related to her friends by seeming to comply with what she thought they might want from her. In reality, this meant that she was often subduing her own desires to fit in with them, although inside she might be seething with resentment at having to do things their way. She would let this continue for a long time until some incident would occur which for her was "the final straw" and she would then turn on them and explain how she really felt, often in a shrill or overly-harsh manner. Her friend would usually be shocked and hurt by her unexpected outburst and often an argument would ensue because this was the first time that Claire had actually let her friend into "her" world and it was very different from the one she had let them see up until that moment. I encouraged Claire to look at things from her friend's perspective and maybe try to be more open with them from the very start. She said, "How can I overwhelm someone with all my stuff when we're just getting to know each other?" I commented that she did not have to overwhelm them but just explain how she liked to socialize and meet new people but could become over-stimulated or exhausted and needed quiet time to herself to recharge her batteries. She was in an almost perpetual battle between wanting company but finding company too draining or demanding.

Her fundamental need for attachment kept her clinging on to some people who she felt gave her energy and she said she used to "ride on their coat tails." She dared not refuse invitations in case she was never asked again. On the other hand, she sometimes found that on the day of the event she was too exhausted or too depressed to attend. If she cancelled at the last minute then she was in danger of letting that friend down and risking the entire friendship. Due to this fear, she often went out without really wanting to and then felt cross and frustrated because she would have preferred to stay home doing something else or just resting. She would then arrive home even more exhausted or depressed, and feeling even more of a failure than ever at her inability to sustain relationships.

Claire's attitude towards her family was equally painful. Of her three brothers she seemed fondest of Patrick, her second sibling, ("the quare fellow") who sounded the kindest but who was also an alcoholic, who drifted in and out of jobs as a chef and only turned up when he needed money or somewhere to stay. She did keep in touch with him, unlike her two brothers who had given up on him years ago.

Her oldest brother had been a teacher and she described him as being quite abrasive and difficult to live with. As a teenager he had once had an argument with their father and they never spoke again – right up until their father died. Although he was married and had children, Claire said that he and his wife led separate lives despite living under the same roof. Claire was fond of her nieces and nephews and got on well with her two sisters-in-law but said there was not much of a relationship with either of her other two brothers. She also said she felt that her sisters-in-law regarded her family as odd and she often felt in the position of having to defend them – and once again felt an outsider.

Claire had been closest to her youngest brother when growing up but said he did not seem to care about her now. She described how hurt she was one Christmas holiday when she went back to Ireland to stay with her cousin Angela and was due to visit this brother on Christmas Day. He did not offer to collect her from the station on Christmas Eve and she had no idea how to get to his house. Eventually, Angela drove her there after a carol service, even though it was a long journey. She was staying in her older brother's house while they were away. She felt so abandoned and rejected that, even though she spent most of Christmas Day and Boxing Day with her brother, she felt isolated and unwanted. On her return to London she fell into a deep depression. She was seeing me at this time so was able to talk through her feelings. She told me how she had felt betrayed by her brother, echoing her sense of betrayal by her mother when she was a child. Claire never allowed herself to be moved to tears in any of our sessions but at this time her pain was palpable and I could sense the unshed tears behind the anger she *was* able to express. In the past she had always gone home at Christmas time and stayed with her parents and had felt looked after and cosseted, which was what she wanted. Since their deaths she had never felt looked after in the same way. She said she just wanted to be somewhere where she did not have to worry about anything, knowing all her needs would be met.

Christmas time was always difficult for Claire as she never knew where she would go or who she would be spending it with; she used to start worrying about Christmas towards the end of October. Usually, she went to Ireland and stayed either with her cousin Angela or one of her brothers but generally came home feeling unsatisfied and would often sink into depression during January. In the second year of therapy, she had gone to the funeral of an aunt and met up again with a cousin she had not seen for many years. This cousin, Brendan, was very friendly towards her and remembered spending childhood holidays with her family. They kept in touch and he invited her to spend a weekend with him and his wife, and Claire deliberated for some time about whether to accept this invitation. Eventually, she accepted and quite enjoyed the weekend as nothing much was expected of her. However, they did not share many interests and she was not sure what to talk about. This triggered feelings from the past of not fitting in and not belonging and not knowing how much of her company people actually wanted. Nevertheless, they subsequently invited her to spend Christmas with them, which she happily accepted so that she did not have to rely on waiting for an invitation from one of her brothers. Although she did not look forward to the holiday with much enthusiasm she said it was pleasant enough and at least she had no feelings of rejection or isolation. It sounded as though they had made her very welcome and although nothing particularly exciting happened, as they spent most of the time watching television in between eating, she was able to go out on her own for walks or read in her room. She came home from that Christmas break feeling less depressed than usual and was able to go into the New Year feeling more hopeful and optimistic about the coming year.

Claire often complained of never being able to have time off, always being "on the treadmill" with no respite when she could let go of the reins and let someone else take all the responsibility. I think this was due to the fact that she was always putting on an adult façade and having to subdue the child part of herself, who was longing to be heard and seen but never being given that chance to show herself. She often felt resentful if she was expected to take charge in any way or make any big decisions and she would tell me stories of events that happened when she was engaged in her driving work for the charity where she had been left to deal with things on her own. She could not understand her own attitude and did not know why she felt so angry when these things occurred. I wondered with her whether this unwillingness was due to the fact that she was always left to look after herself and therefore did not want the extra responsibility of looking after others as well. There were so many occasions when Claire was left in a "Catch 22" situation where, as she often said herself, "I'm damned if I do and damned if I don't."

After some time, when I had experienced her anger many times, I saw that anger was one of the few emotions she felt free to express. This anger was the top layer under which there bubbled a cauldron of grief, despair and deep hurt but these more painful feelings were much harder for Claire to access, and so became channelled into the anger, which was the only way in which she could let them out.

Claire evoked in me similar feelings to those evoked by my father throughout my life. He had been a difficult man to live with and was someone for whom nothing could ever be right. I could never please him, however hard I tried, and was always left feeling inadequate, useless and somehow "wanting" and at fault. This was exactly the way Claire made me feel on many occasions when she accused me of not really understanding her, mis-attuning and missing the point. Also, on the rare occasions when I did get things right or made her feel understood or sufficiently soothed, she found it extremely hard to acknowledge. This, too, was reminiscent of my father who would only ever grudgingly thank me for something. So, I had to be vigilant and aware of what was happening regarding this counter-transference.

Claire's feeling of intense loneliness permeated many of our sessions, where I felt we were both stranded on separate desert islands and could not meet, however hard I tried to swim over to her and land on her island's shore. Occasionally, I was allowed onto her island and we could sit together on the beach and look at the world together, but more often than not we were separated by some unbridgeable gap that I was always trying to step over. I keenly felt Claire's deep deprivation and hurt of such magnitude that she dared not look at it too closely herself. There was one point during the therapy, after she had returned from a three-week holiday, when she fell into yet another deep depression and for the first time contemplated suicide. She said she had never seriously considered that before but now understood why some people felt compelled to take their own lives. I was left feeling more inadequate than ever and that I had truly failed her. During the session in which she told me this, she was wearing a pretty pink, black-and-white necklace, a very rare occurrence. I could not help thinking that if she had been feeling that suicidal she would not have bothered to put on this adornment. Normally she wore no jewellery at all. I was puzzled by the difference between what she was saying and how she was presenting herself. In my mind I had come to think of her as "Mary, Mary Quite Contrary".

One of the stories Claire told me about her childhood exemplified the attitude that her parents took towards her. It happened when she was seven and her parents were out for the afternoon. She was being looked after by Bridie. Suddenly an ambulance stopped outside their house and two people came in to say they had come to take her to hospital to have her tonsils taken out. Neither she nor Bridie knew anything about this so they had to scramble around finding pyjamas and other things for her to take with her to hospital. Her parents had deliberately withheld this information because they knew from past experience that she would be upset and not wish to go. So they decided to go out and say nothing about it in order that she would not have the chance to get upset beforehand. She was taken to hospital in Dublin for two weeks, on her own, and neither of her parents visited during the time she was there. She remembers the feelings of abandonment, helplessness, fear, homesickness and complete shattering of her trust in them. After that episode, she gave up on getting anything back from her mother, whom she always blamed as being the main instigator, and knew that she only had herself to rely on in the future.

Another incident occurred when she was ten, when she had accompanied both her parents to Dublin for the afternoon. She and her mother went shopping and had agreed to meet her father later. Her mother had some kind of a panic attack and could not find the way back, so Claire had to take over, look after her mother and find where they had arranged to meet her father. She felt a mixture of irritation with her mother, coupled with anxiety about finding her father again. I felt this said a great deal about her subsequent reluctance to take charge in situations and her impatience with people who needed looking after.

The accumulation of these kinds of incidents all helped to forge Claire's personality, explaining so much about her inability to trust other people or even to warm to them and certainly never to entrust them with her deepest feelings. I felt she started to build up her carapace of self-sufficiency from a very early age and protected her vulnerability by shielding it from the world, carefully shrouding it, so that no one could ever guess how desperately she needed comfort, companionship and warmth. She had no real secure base to return to so her whole life was built on the shakiest of foundations, which meant it often crumbled and she was left to pick up the pieces once again and start over.

All this meant that Claire's attitude towards me was ambivalent at best and hostile at worst. After the first few months of therapy, she was sharply critical of any interpretations or attempts on my part to shed light on why she behaved the way she did. She would often dismiss my thoughts as irrelevant or as ones she had already discovered for herself, so that I was not telling her anything she did not already know. She would also bully me from time to time and even acknowledged that she did so. Sometimes, it was difficult to be patient with her but patience was a lesson I had been learning throughout my life from my dealings with my father, other difficult-to-please male figures from places of work and from looking after Frances. If there was one thing I was not short of, it was patience. It was also quite difficult to like Claire as she could sometimes be deliberately spiteful and say things that I was pretty sure she knew were hurtful. She told me she used to do this with her mother when she was an adolescent and had even reduced her mother to tears at times. It would have helped if I had detected a sense of humour in Claire but she seemed remarkably short of humour, not surprising as there was not much in her life to be amused by. However, there were moments when we found ourselves smiling or laughing together.

Despite all this, Claire came regularly for her sessions, hardly ever missing one, and if she was ill she would request a telephone session instead. I accommodated her wishes for changes to the days and times of her sessions and would always ring her back promptly if she left me a message. We also began to talk about books. Two inroads I had found into her world were books and art, both of which we would discuss occasionally. The main focus of each session was herself and her reactions to others, her difficulties at work and with relationships, her feelings of isolation and loneliness, her inability to tolerate more than a modicum of intrusion, and her feelings of becoming overwhelmed and "taken over" by others. As time went on she also became annoyed at her dependence on coming to see me, even though she said I did not give her what she was really seeking. She did grudgingly admit that coming to "offload" was helping her.

During one of our earliest sessions I commented that it seemed as though Claire had been almost invisible to everyone while she was growing up and she agreed with this. I felt that part of our work together was to enable her to become visible again, not only to other people but also to herself. She was so unsure of who she really was and had so little sense of self that many of our sessions were taken up with allowing her to show who she truly was, expressing her own views to me without censure or worry about who she might be upsetting or offending. At first she found this difficult and would often speak hesitatingly with many pauses and long silences. However, as time went on she began to find her voice and during some sessions would speak most eloquently and fluently, letting me see parts of her that she had hidden from the world for decades. Often this felt like bloodletting as streams of anger, resentment, spite and bile poured out of her as though she was squeezing inflamed spots to let the pus drain away. Despite doing this on a regular basis, she still had to go back and pick at those sore spots. Occasionally though, she would say that being allowed to express her anger and frustration and disappointment was helpful.

I knew that Claire really wanted the companionship of a significant other but was too wary to entrust anyone with her deepest feelings or allow them to get near to her. Alan B Eppel (2009) says: "with intimacy comes a fear of vulnerability, the threat of losing one's identity or autonomy". Another of Claire's problems was her fear of being inauthentic. She was a smoker but rarely let her friends know this. She felt she was betraying herself by smoking when, as an acupuncturist, she ought really to be living the kind of life she advocated for her patients. However, she had no wish to give up smoking so it was done in secret with much misgiving and a feeling of both defiance and guilt. She knew a few other smokers, so would smoke in their company, but this lack of allowing other people to know about her smoking habit left her feeling a fraud and thereby inauthentic.

There were a few occasions when Claire did seem to appreciate what was happening in the therapy and one Monday she arrived bearing a gift for me. It was a piece of cake from one she had baked at the weekend. It was wrapped in tinfoil and she said she did not know if I ate cake but she wanted me to have some. This was at a time when I had been going through great personal stress and had lost a considerable amount of weight. I wondered if this was Claire's way of addressing that without actually saying anything to me about the weight loss. When I did eventually put some weight back on she commented that I looked much better and that she thought I had been too thin before. I accepted the cake and thanked her for it but then had to pay a heavy price for this present. For the next few sessions she was harder to please than ever and rejected almost everything I said to her and questioned whether or not I even listened properly to her. Our sessions seemed to be an intellectual battleground, with one or other of us batting words backwards and forwards in an attempt to make the other one see our point of view. Eventually, we reached an impasse and Claire said she could no longer think of anything to say to me. I made her forget what she was trying to say, made her forget her train of thought and talked too much so that she became distracted. We sat in uncomfortable silence for some time until at last Claire was able to find her voice again. But we survived that particular battle and moved on to a different battleground. Every aspect of therapy appeared to involve a tussle in whichever area we were exploring. I appreciated what a struggle Claire's life was for her, how often she had felt embattled and besieged in her own existence. It took many defeats and a few triumphs for Claire to come out in her true colours and declare herself, to show me the person so carefully shrouded by the different veils she had wrapped round herself for most of her life. Each unwrapping was painful and made her feel so vulnerable and exposed, open to criticism and blame and shame.

During the few times when she seemed happier and more able to cope with life and relationships, she always found something to worry about and said to me she "nearly always sabotages things when it all looks as though it's going well." We were then able to discuss how change can be really scary when everything seems unfamiliar and almost unnatural. A significant change seemed to take place after about 27 months of therapy. Claire was able to challenge her cousin Angela, with whom she had had the longest and most intimate relationship of her life, about Angela's talkativeness and the fact that she rarely allowed others (namely Claire) the space in which to talk about themselves. This opened up into a really deep discussion about honesty and openness, after which Claire felt as though she had released a huge burden. She said that she was able to tell Angela how misunderstood she had felt by her for many years and how Angela's perception of her childhood did not match with her own view. Angela was fond of saying that Claire's childhood had been fine, that she had been better off financially than many other children and that her relationships with her parents and brothers had been quite normal. Claire was at last able to explain to Angela the isolation in which they had all lived, hardly communicating with each other on anything other than the most superficial level, and how feelings were never discussed.

After this frank talk she was able to sleep well that night, whereas she said that Angela later told her she had lain awake for nearly two hours thinking of their discussion. This led to a number of changes in the way they related to each other and thereafter Claire was able to be much more honest with Angela about her feelings. She also felt that for the first time Angela understood her a little better. In the past she had always been made to feel ungrateful for what Angela considered to be her better-than-average start in life, totally unable to comprehend the deep deprivation and lack of empathy that Claire had in fact experienced.

Due to her inner loneliness as a child, and subsequently as an adult, Claire had learned to compensate for her lack of warm friendships and empathic relationships. She turned to solitary pursuits such as bicycling, walking, reading and painting. If she did find friends who shared her enjoyment of these activities then she might meet a friend to go for a walk or cycle ride but found it much more difficult if this extended to more than a one-to-one relationship. Sometimes friends she had invited to join her for a particular activity would bring along another friend, or more than one, and Claire always found this particularly hard, thinking that she was being overlooked or sidelined. We linked this back to how she felt within her family group, being one of four children who was never really listened to or taken notice of or made to feel that she had anything of value to offer and who was often teased or ridiculed if she did try to have her say. She found conversations in these large groups well nigh impossible and I suggested this was due to the fear of being exposed as the vulnerable child she felt like when put in these group situations. It was hard enough for Claire to converse on a one-to-one basis so having a three-way or four-way conversation was often beyond her and she would just let the others talk while she listened. She would then feel frustrated and furious afterwards, just as she had done as a child when she would often go to her room fuming at her inability to make any kind of impression and feeling humiliated by her brothers when she tried.

Claire's life often sounded bleak and joyless and she would describe how she had to plan meals carefully to eke out her money and how she would cook on a Monday so that she had meals for the rest of the week. Any unexpected change to her routine threw her and she often worried about why she did things in such a rigid way. She said she would come home from work, eat her meal and watch television and seemed to think that this was somehow wrong or that other people did much more exciting things with their evenings. We talked about how she set her own parameters as a means of controlling her environment and making her feel safe within it. Again this tapped into her childhood feelings of never being in control of situations, always at the mercy of others.

She had one particular friend she talked about many times. This friend had two teenage children and her home was always in a terrible mess and she complained of money worries, and yet she would be out practically every night doing something new and exciting. Claire was often invited to join her and felt obliged to accept these invitations but always felt that she was not valued for her own company but was just someone to be used as a useful companion. She tried hard to engage this other woman in deep conversations but was often interrupted by outside phone calls or demands by her children or by her friend launching off into some monologue of her own, so the friendship never satisfied Claire's deepest needs. Also this woman was often late, whereas Claire was always punctual, and this was a constant irritation.

After a holiday break for both of us, when we had not seen each other for five weeks, Claire informed me she was hiding behind me and isolating herself from her friends, relying solely on me to listen to her; she felt worried about this and too dependent on me. She had never missed a therapist while on holiday before, but this time she said she could not contain herself when she was on her own and her need for me infuriated her. This enabled us to talk more about her need for attachment and she said for the first time that she felt she had changed slightly since coming to see me. We were able to discuss her growing attachment to me and how this could be a strength not a weakness. In the longer term, having a secure attachment relationship for the first time could, on the contrary, enable her to go out into the world and explore and take risks in letting others get closer to her.

Fourteen months into the therapy my sister died and I had to cancel two sessions. When we resumed, initially Claire was solicitous and gentler than usual with me. However, after a couple of weeks, she sent me a text message one day which I did not receive, so I could not reply. She then tried to phone me but I did not answer. When I eventually answered her later call, she sounded quite stressed and said she felt as though *she* was taking care of *me*. I asked what she meant and she said as she could not get hold of me, she wondered what had happened and listed a whole litany of possibilities – ranging from my having an accident to my house burning down. Then she said she wondered if I had been doing it deliberately as I might think it was therapeutic for her in some way. I asked "doing what deliberately?" and she said, "not being available or contactable." I was quite shocked she could think that and said quite forcibly, "I'm not like that, Claire. I would never do anything so manipulative." She sounded a bit mollified and after a long pause I said it was interesting she should react in such a way. "I knew you'd say that," she said. "It's an easy thing to hide behind." Again, this incident allowed us to examine more closely some of her deepest feelings regarding relationships and how a fear of abandonment underscored so many of her other anxieties. We linked this back to her complicated relationship with her mother, who had looked to Claire to regulate her own feelings from an early age and hardly ever took on the responsibility of looking after Claire's emotional needs. Instead of helping Claire to regulate her feelings by empathising and putting herself in Claire's shoes to help her to understand her own feelings, her mother had used her to soothe her own feelings of inadequacy and need for companionship. We explored the numerous abandonments she had suffered so far in her life and how she had subsequently protected herself from becoming too close or dependent on others for fear of repeating that pain.

After 18 months into the therapy Claire's cousin, Angela, became seriously ill. She had previously suffered from cancer, from which she had recovered, and at first it seemed as though this was a recurrence. She was in hospital, in great pain, on heavy medication and had started a course of chemotherapy. Claire was worried about her but also told me how she admired the way Angela was coping and how she herself would have been unable to cope in the same way. She said that if ever she was seriously ill, she would be very bitter and want to blame someone for it and would certainly not have a positive attitude about it, as Angela did. In fact, Claire said she would feel very sorry for herself and probably just "curl into a ball and wait to die." She also said how there would be no one who would really miss her if she was gone. It was discovered that Angela was not suffering from cancer but a serious infection in a bone, for which she was treated over a long period. Eventually she came out of hospital, walking with the aid of a stick, and her attitude was that she had been spared death and was happily grateful for her life and determined to make the most of it. Claire said that she would have been furious at the initial misdiagnosis and the months of pain and worry, and then dismayed at having to learn to walk again and pick up the pieces of her life and carry on as normal.

This whole episode led us to talking very deeply about Claire's concerns regarding her own mortality and whether or not she had wasted her life. She had vivid memories of her mother towards the end of her life, living alone and refusing help from anyone until she had to move into a care home. She remembered thinking how alone her mother was and hoping she would not finish up in the same way.

Some months after Angela's discharge from hospital she told Claire that she was going to become a grandmother and that, as her daughter lived in London, she would be visiting more frequently. Claire's feelings about this were, as usual, ambivalent but she seemed pleased whenever Angela rang and invited herself to stay, as her daughter did not have enough room. Claire was never sure if Angela chose to stay with her for her own sake or just because it was convenient. However, on the occasions when Angela came to stay, Claire enjoyed the company and said she felt better for the fact that there was someone waiting at home when she returned from work, and she could talk to her about her day and share things with her. She liked being able to cook for them and repay some of the hospitality that Angela had always shown her over the years. After the baby was born Angela came to stay quite frequently and, although she visited her daughter and new baby grandson during the day, she would be there in the evenings and Claire was happy for her to stay.

After two years of therapy, Claire requested going down to just one session a week and we agreed to start this but it did not work out. For the first three weeks of this arrangement she found it necessary to call me between sessions and was very angry with me during our sessions. It was clear that she could not manage on just one session a week. I suggested going back to two sessions and we compromised by having one phone session and one session where we met.

At the end of two-and-a-half years I could see changes in Claire but it took her somewhat longer to acknowledge any of these. I found her becoming more open about her feelings, more willing to talk about the things that troubled her without brooding on them for so long, and more accepting of other people and their different approaches and ways of doing things. There was a certain softening of her intolerance to some people and a greater tolerance of their own needs that did not necessarily conflict with hers any longer. She seemed happier to acknowledge that other people might even feel the same way as she did but had different ways of expressing it. There was one occasion in therapy where I started the session by telling Claire how I felt she reacted to certain situations by giving up very easily, saying to herself, "Oh, what's the point?" and then we talked of other things. At the end of this session, Claire stated that she would have liked me to point out that she gave up hope too quickly. I was a bit taken aback and reminded her of what I had said at the start of the session but she countered this with, "But you didn't use the same words as I did." I looked at her for a moment and saw the funny side of this and started to laugh. She looked at me and then started to laugh as well. We finished the session laughing together as Claire realised that we were on the same side after all.

After three-and-a-half years Claire had changed quite radically. She had managed to cut down on coming to see me to once a week and this had been successful for six months. For the final three months she reduced to once a fortnight, a gradual weaning off process that seemed the safest way to end this particular therapy. Her relationships with her friends had become much easier as she was able to show more tolerance towards them and was also able to express her own needs more often. She was enjoying work more because she felt at ease and happier in her own skin and realised that she was offering a service that helped other people, and was often told how grateful they were for her help. She no longer felt burdened by a pervasive sense of sadness and doom, a feeling that had been with her most of her life. This shroud had lifted and she felt optimistic about life. She was content with her life at home in her little flat, which she had completely redecorated during the last few months of therapy. She told me happily about the changes she had made at home and these reflected the inner changes that had taken place.

So what was it that facilitated the process of change in Claire? I think initially it was my capacity to stay grounded in the face of her repeated attempts to wreck the therapy. The growth of her attachment to me caused a lot of upheaval in her inner world. Dissonance was created by the harsh expectations laid down in her early internal working model set against my empathy, interest and patience. I had already learnt in the relationship with my father that no matter what I did, I could not please him; I think this was counter-transferentially repeated in my relationship with Claire, who apparently resisted all my therapeutic efforts. I expressed my feelings of frustration and helplessness in supervision but, as my awareness of this dynamic grew, so did my need to get off the treadmill. There was no more I could do to please her. Paradoxically, it was this understanding that gave me greater freedom in my interactions with Claire and allowed me to challenge her more often. This was reflected in our both being able to laugh at her complaints that "I did not use the same words." She was now ready to look at the impact of her negativity on her relationships in general plus I had become visible as a real person and not simply as a "creature of her projections". But this only happened as a result of the groundwork I had already put in of consistency, and the attunement I attempted during the gruelling first two-and-a-half years of therapy. It was the building of a "secure attachment" relationship with me (her first ever), and Claire taking this in, that enabled her to recover – to feel safer inside, safer to explore in the world and relate to others without needing them to be her mother.

Claire's therapy was like walking through a dense wood. It was overcast with huge dark trees looming above us. Occasionally shafts of sunlight illuminated the gloom and occasionally we reached open glades where the sun shone fiercely from a pitiless sky, making Claire's sharp black shadow stretch in front of us, but most of the time we stumbled along together, tripping over tree roots and fallen branches, trying to find the right path.

# Chapter 4

# Reclaiming love

Our younger son was born in the early hours of a Friday morning. He came into this world quickly, just two hours after we arrived at the hospital, and he greeted the world silently with a look of astonishment. He lay back with his arms above his head and looked around him in wonderment as if to say, "Where is this? What just happened?" His black hair was smooth around his head as though he had spent his final moments in the womb brushing it. After a few seconds he looked at me and his big brown eyes locked onto mine as if he had always known me. Then he made a little cry, a soft greeting. The midwife helped me scoop him up and I held him close. He has been close to my heart ever since. He was a beautiful baby, often mistaken for a girl for the first two years of his life. In character he was so unlike his elder brother that it was quite a culture shock. He was quiet and dreamy and would amuse himself in his cot before calling out for me. He would lie back and lazily tap his foot against the activity centre attached to the side of the cot, so different from his brother who used to play with it enthusiastically making everything ring and rotate and rattle. I remember once taking a friend, who had visited me after dropping her children at school, upstairs to see him thinking he was still asleep. However, he was wide awake, lying in his cot staring solemnly at us from between the bars. She looked at him and said, "Oooh, he's been here before, hasn't he?"

Whereas our elder son was an extremely active toddler needing to be taken out to play every day, running, jumping, climbing, skipping and always on the go, our younger son was equally happy to sit and play with toys and jigsaws, to look at books or just stare out of the window at the leaves on the trees and the clouds in the sky. As a baby, our elder son used to love being put in his baby bouncer and I could keep an eye on him there for a while as I cooked or did some ironing and he would jump up and down kicking his legs happily. Our younger son, on the other hand, used to sit in it and occasionally bounce up and down a bit and then look at me with a bored expression as if to say, "What do you want me to do in here?" I did not let him stay in it for more than ten minutes at a time. He used to sit on his baby mat and direct his brother to fetch him toys. Our elder son crawled at six months and whizzed around our flat like a little dynamo. Our younger did not crawl early, except for a desultory commando-style crawling that he mastered at about a year. He clearly found this much too like hard work and soon found his feet and walked instead. It took our elder son longer to walk, as he was so adept at crawling it did not seem to occur to him to get up on his feet. They both talked early though, probably because I talked to them so much, and we were able to have proper conversations from an early age. It fascinated me that their characters and personalities were so clear from birth. How much was inherited and how much was due to their environment, I wondered.

Part of my psychotherapy training involved 18 months of "infant observation" and I was lucky enough to observe a much loved little boy, the third child in his family. His mother was well-attuned to him and having already had two children she knew what she was doing and had a relaxed attitude. The other two children were somewhat older than him, being 12 and 10 when he was born. She had suffered an ectopic pregnancy five years earlier and really wanted this third child. I observed him from when he was just a few days old until he reached 18 months, so I could see how he responded to the world and became attached to his parents and siblings throughout his pre-verbal stage. I came to visit once a week for an hour, and the mother and I developed a close relationship. This essential part of my training taught me so much and I believe is invaluable in any psycho-therapeutic training. It taught me to watch every nuance of body language and facial expression. The words people use are extremely important in psychotherapy but the silences and the unspoken words are equally important.

# Petros

One man I worked with for just over three years came to see me about his depression, his extremely poor relationship with his mother and his ambivalence about his sexuality. When I first asked him to tell me about himself, he said he had already achieved what he set out to do in life, which was to get a good education, do work that he enjoyed, live somewhere nice and own a car. He said he was not particularly materialistic, so was not bothered about doing any better. He had a partner, with whom he felt a deep connection, but he was not especially interested in sex and never had been. They did not live together. He also had some close women friends and was still on good terms with previous partners, apart from one with whom he felt he had wasted six months of his life.

Petros was an exceptionally good-looking young man, tall and athletic with dark brown hair and deep blue eyes. He was in his 30s, of Mediterranean origin and had a Greek father and a German mother. His mother was much closer with his older sister and they often used to shut themselves away in the kitchen chatting, locking the door so he could not interrupt. I expressed surprise at this and said, "They actually locked the door? Not just closed it?" and he said, "Yes, I remember trying to open it but it was locked." I said how sad I thought that was and he nodded. He was a solitary child who did not have many friends. He would visit them at their houses but felt somewhat ashamed to invite them back to his home, as they lived in a small and cramped flat, albeit in a wealthy area. He remembered going to nursery school and crying when his mother left him, but said it was a nice school with a big garden with a peach tree in it. Once he started primary school he did well immediately and knew at once that the only way to escape his life was to work hard and leave home as soon as he could.

Petros excelled in every subject and his mother did not bother to attend parent-teacher evenings after the first few years, as he always did so well that she never felt the need. His sister often used to go instead, just to sign that they had received his reports. His father never visited his school. His father was a sea captain and would be away for months at a time and would come home for a couple of months each year. Before he came home a black cloud would descend, as his mother clearly did not want him around. They slept in separate rooms. Petros made an effort to get to know his father better when he had grown up, and realised that he had been influenced by his mother's attitude towards his dad. He continued to do very well at school and decided to study physics at university with a view to teaching it. His mother had wanted him to study medicine and his father wanted him to do civil engineering, but as he won scholarships all the way he felt they had no right to dictate what he should do. He decided to take his Masters degree in England, for which he also won a scholarship, and then went on to do a PhD. He was delighted to come to England and the only thing he missed about home was the weather. When he started seeing me, he was working in a responsible job in a well known London hospital.

Petros recalled that when he was about seven and playing football, he was running after the ball when he suddenly thought: "Why am I doing this? Why are we all running after a ball like this? There is no point to it and it is a ridiculous activity." So he dropped out of the game and stood at the side. Looking back, he could not understand why he did not just carry on and enjoy the game. He admitted that he often felt other people were rather stupid but he held back from expressing his views, as he did not want people to think he was arrogant. He also often felt that other people were quite lazy, as he had learned from an early age that if he really wanted to get on then he had to knuckle down and master whatever subject he was studying. He put in the work and was dismissive of others who were not so committed.

He described a rather bleak and cheerless childhood with a controlling mother who was determined that her children should do well. She rationed the time they spent watching television, was very strict about the kind of food they ate, allowing no sugar or treats, and did not allow Petros or his sister to sit around "doing nothing". If she found them idle she would send them to play outside. As an adult, Petros said he had a weakness for cakes and sweets, having been deprived of them as a child. He said he could never relax and just "be", as he always needed to be doing something constructive and felt uncomfortable if he was not busy. He had also known from an early age that he was attracted to boys rather than girls. He had been in a few relation-ships and said he liked the intimacy, kissing and cuddling, but found sex itself completely unsatisfying. He had even tried going to prostitutes to see if it would be any better with a woman, but it still left him unmoved. This was causing a problem with his present boyfriend of over two years. They were sexually incompatible as he was not really interested in sex and found many excuses to avoid it. He had also never lived with anyone else and could not imagine doing so. He valued his own space and thought he would feel "invaded" if he had to share it. He lived in a house that he shared with an ex-partner but they had separate rooms; he felt obliged to stay with him because he knew this man had many problems and he had once saved him from suicide. He felt responsible for him and thought that if he left to move elsewhere then his friend would try to take his own life again.

We looked more closely at his "dismissive" attitude and I commented that in fact he had been treated very dismissively by his mother (locking him out of the kitchen, not taking notice of his views) so was it surprising that he had developed a dismissive attitude himself? He sat back and thought about this quietly for a few minutes and then said, "That's almost too simplistic, isn't it?" I said that maybe it was but it seemed a simple matter of repeating what had been done to him. He then gave me a few examples of how his mother had emotionally punished him as a child. He said she was against physical punishment but he would rather have been smacked by her than made to feel guilty and ashamed of having hurt her or let her down. We discussed how she had been forced to be both mother and father and he said that she was not much good at either role. In fact, he said that from an early age he thought that neither of his parents was much good at their job of parenting. After he left, I decided that his was going to be a challenging therapy, as I guessed that my views were going to be "dismissed" and I was going to be thought of as stupid and, possibly, lazy.

When Petros arrived the next week, he told me that on the drive home from the last session he had been thinking about how much he had opened up to me and how grateful he felt for meeting someone he could talk to about everything. He suddenly wondered what would happen if I were to pass away and he started to cry. He told me he had not cried for about seven years and this completely took him by surprise. Sometimes he had wanted to be able to cry but had never managed to do so. I asked him who he had turned to as a child when he felt upset or worried; he thought about this and eventually said, "I had no one to turn to so I just dealt with it myself. When I got older I used to take a text book with me and walk along the beach, for hours, and I would talk in my head to God – so I suppose he was the one I confided in most. It's funny now because I no longer really believe, but then I did." He also told me of how attached he became to objects, particular pencils he liked, for instance, and how upset he would become if he lost one. He later told me that when he watched television now, he sat with his toy animal collection around him, about 15 soft toys that he had collected over the years. He blushed as he related this and said he would never let anyone else know such a thing, as he knew how odd it must seem to anyone else, a grown man in his 30s surrounded by cuddly toys. I felt sad that he had to rely on those toys for comfort and security.

He said he never remembered his mother cuddling or kissing him. He recalled an occasion when he was about seven when he was walking with his mother along the beach and he told her that he loved her. She laughed at him and said, "You won't say that when you're a teenager." He felt deeply rejected by her answer, and wondered why she had said that and could not just accept his offer of love to her. However, he acknowledged that when he became a teenager he realised that his mother had been right. He also said that she was often sending him off to play in other friends' houses. At the time he had thought this was a rejection of him. When he spoke about this to her much later she said it was her way of getting him to socialise more, because she was concerned that he was too introspective and solitary. He also saw that his friends were much more affectionate with their mothers, climbing onto their laps or being kissed or stroked by them, and it puzzled him as he never saw anything like this at home; he had decided that they were all "odd". Now he thought differently.

He used to telephone his mother about once every three weeks, sometimes not as often as that. He felt bad about it, because she was getting older and they often quarrelled when they spoke. However, he did not know how to make their relationship better. He said he did not want her to die before they had established a closer relationship. This was something we worked on throughout his therapy and it helped him when we explored his mother's own background which had been harsh and unloving. She had been brought up by a single mother in Germany during the war, with no luxuries and very little love. Her father had died when she was little and her mother had to work hard to bring her up. She was used to having little money and making do and eking things out, and had been taught that life was hard and tough and one just had to get on with it. There was no time for sentiment or feelings. She had never been lovingly mothered herself, so had no idea of how that was done. She also had no siblings to share anything with, material or emotional. She was on her own and ultimately made her children feel the same way.

After some months of discussing his mother's background, Petros said he now understood more about the effect his mother's attitude had towards him and the fact that his father had very little influence over him, leaving him to absorb the atmosphere in his family home and the malign feelings engendered by his mother. He now realised that she felt inadequate and insecure and managed to do better for his sister, but really did not understand little boys or what they needed. She thought that they required a lot of direction, discipline and controlling, whereas if she had just managed to love him then he may have turned out better equipped to face life. He now felt that she had such a deficit of love in her own life that she found it hard to give him any, except in the way she thought would be useful. He no longer felt the resentment he used to have towards her but was sad that it could not have been different.

His mother had visited Greece as a teenager and fallen in love with a handsome sea captain, stayed and married him. She did not return to Germany until after her husband's death. Petros told me that his father had died suddenly and unexpectedly a few years earlier and he was quite relieved that he never had to have the conversation with him about his own sexuality, as he knew it would have been difficult. So far he had not yet told his mother about his sexuality and she never asked him about personal matters, only questions about his work or general things. His sister had guessed, but was leaving it to him to tell their mother and he did not know if he ever would or could. His sister was married and had four children, but he thought their marriage was "on the rocks" as his brother-in-law did not give his sister all the things she craved, and he recognised that his sister despised her husband. He described her as spoilt and selfish. He told me about unkind and intrusive things she had done while they were growing up and, although they maintained a civilised relationship as adults, he did not seem to regard her with much affection. He took his role as an uncle seriously and sometimes commented on the way she was bringing up her children, as he did not always approve of it. He had strong views on how children ought to be raised, mostly different from his own upbringing.

Over the next few months the focus was more on his relationship with his boyfriend and he felt it was inevitable they would split up, for a number of reasons, one of them being their sexual incompatibility. He said he might consider trying a relationship with a woman, because he had never really enjoyed sex with either a man or a woman, so if he found a woman who was not particularly bothered about having a physical relationship, but did want children, then they might have a good partnership. He did have a hankering for children and a family life. We spoke about this at some length, as I was concerned that if he followed that path, he might then meet a man to whom he was attracted which would jeopardise any relationship he was in with a woman. He said he would have to be totally honest with a woman right at the start of a relationship and explain his position. He understood this presented considerable obstacles but felt that some women would still be happy with the situation, in order to have children and a partner. He commented that heterosexual couples were often tempted outside of marriage and had affairs.

Eventually he did split up with his boyfriend after a number of upsetting experiences, but subsequently met a new man. At the same time, he was applying for more responsible jobs abroad and had been accepted for one in an Arab country. This presented its own difficulties, as he was naturally concerned about being a homosexual in an Arab country. After discussing this with various friends he felt that if he was discreet then it should not pose too much of a problem and the worst that could happen might be that he was deported. In fact, he had never let any co-workers know about his sexuality, as he did not want to be the subject of gossip. He was not at all camp, which was one of the problems he had had with his previous boyfriend; he had felt that when they were out together everyone would know about their relationship, as his boyfriend was decidedly camp. He wanted people he worked with to believe he was straight and he cultivated friendships with female colleagues to make this more believable. He knew that some of the women he worked with fancied him and he did not want to put them off.

It took him some time to get over his break-up with his boyfriend, who had been unfaithful among other things, and he told me that he still felt anger towards him for having caused him such pain; then at times he just felt sadness that their relationship had not worked. He began to develop a new friendship and it was quite a departure for him, as the man was nearer in age to him, instead of much younger as his last boyfriend had been, or much older as his previous relationships had been. He said he had learnt a lot over the time he had spent in therapy and was more open with his new boyfriend than he had been in the past. He was pleased to find that old friends of his took to the new man in his life, whereas they had never felt that he was suited to his last boyfriend, and this boosted his confidence in his own judgement. He even began to talk of them moving in together, which would have been the first time for him to share his life and home with someone else.

At the same time he was offered a prestigious job in the Arab country and it was too good an offer to refuse. His boyfriend understood his situation and began to look for work in the same place, so that they could still be together. The next few months were busy for Petros, as he thought through the implications of the new job, but eventually he moved abroad to take up the position and we continued our therapy via Skype. It was difficult for him to settle into the new country because everything was so different, he felt a bit isolated and he also found it a huge culture shock. He was dismayed by the attitudes he encountered, such as using domestic help almost as slaves, and the fact that women had to be totally covered up and had so many restrictions put upon them. However, it was not as difficult in some ways as he had feared. In fact, it was easy to mix with other men without suspicion, as the sexes were so segregated anyway. He was surprised that the laws of the country were easily flouted as long as it was done discreetly.

He was now much more financially rewarded and could afford to send his mother more money, and pay for her to come over and visit him. This visit proved a turning point for them, as he was at last able to talk to her about his emotionally deprived childhood. She apologised for not having been the kind of mother he needed at the time, but said that she had done the best she could, and he believed her. She told him how proud she was of him, and how she always had been, even though he had thought he was never able to please her. He even had the courage to tell her that he was gay, and to his immense surprise and relief she accepted it and told him she had thought so for quite a while.

At around this time he met a man to whom he became very close and eventually, after much soul-searching on his part, their relationship became a sexual one. It was a mutually rewarding relationship and he confessed that this was the first time he had ever felt sexually satisfied and happy, so he believed that he had just never met "the right one" before. He acknowledged that he would be hurting the boyfriend who had eased his pain after his previous break-up, but felt that this had been a rebound relationship and that the man would understand. He did regret betraying this other man's love and trust in him; the man was indeed very upset with Petros when he learnt about the new relationship but was not entirely surprised. He had anticipated that this might happen once Petros moved to another country.

Soon after this Petros decided to finish therapy, saying he had learnt a great deal from it, and thanked me for "giving me my mother back." He said he felt so comfortable with his new partner that he could discuss whatever issues he wanted to with him. This man was warm, sensible and understanding; Petros felt closer to him than any other person he had ever known, and he was seriously considering them living together. He seemed much happier than when he first came to see me and had resolved many issues that had plagued him throughout his life, due to a fuller understanding of the emotional neglect he had suffered throughout his childhood and adolescence. Exploring his background and his past behaviour, without fear of judgement or disapproval, had allowed him to adjust the way he approached relationships. It had given him the confidence to embark on a new relationship in an open-hearted way and to talk to his mother honestly, with forgiveness and respect, allowing them to forge a new and mutually loving relationship with each other.

# Chapter 5

# Therapy with an elderly couple

Sometimes being a therapist can take one to extremely painful places. We meet someone whose story is so poignant that listening to it can be almost unbearable, yet they have to bear it and so must we. One such therapy was with a couple, both in their 80s. This therapy was rooted in the very essence of attachment; the feelings we have for those closest to us, the bonds that have deepened through years of loving each other and the unbearable feelings of pain when we lose someone. It was unusual because it did not cover many of the "usual" areas of therapy, namely examining past patterns of behaviour in an endeavour to change them for the better, scrutinising our attachment history to see why we have reacted in certain ways during our life, helping someone to resolve deep issues so that they can go on to live a happier life. No, this therapy was more about acceptance and understanding, remembering and relinquishing.

## Alfred and Janet

Alfred was 84 when I first started to see him. He had suffered a stroke two years before which had left him in a wheelchair. This was one aspect of the therapy but the main reason for him seeking help was more traumatic. One of his grandchildren, Michael, had committed suicide when he was aged just 21. Alfred was finding it extremely difficult to take this on board and had become withdrawn and depressed, sometimes not speaking all day. His wife and their four children all decided that he needed therapy and had approached their GP who initiated the process.

Alfred's stroke had affected his left side and he could no longer walk. On my first visit Janet, his wife, let me in and led me into their back sitting room. The downstairs front room was now Alfred's bedroom. He was sitting in a wheelchair facing the back garden. His left arm was hunched up on his chest. He had white hair, wore glasses and a hearing aid. His speech was unaffected. He was sitting upright and looked somewhat thinner than in a photograph I saw of him in the room, obviously taken some years previously. He asked if Janet could sit in on the session as he said he did not always remember things that well.

He began by telling me about his stroke and how he was coping. He then said that four months after having a stroke (he was in hospital for two months), his grandson Michael, aged 21, had committed suicide. No one knew why he did that and he gave no indication beforehand. He and Janet had four children and Michael was the middle son of their oldest daughter. Michael had an older brother, John, and a younger brother, James, who was about to start university. He and James had been particularly close. I expressed my sincere condolences and said that no parent or grandparent should ever have to go through something like that. During this session he gave me some biographical details about growing up in Shoreditch, the oldest of three children with one younger brother, who had died five years ago, and one younger sister, who had emigrated to Australia many years ago but now lived in America.

Alfred then told me some incidents from his childhood. Once, when he was two years old, he was playing with his cousin, Robert, who was a similar age to him, in their grandparents' garden and he found the rusty spoke of an old umbrella. He started to suck it and Robert tried to pull it away from him and it tore his mouth and throat. He was taken to the doctor, who treated it but it became infected; he had to go to hospital because the inside of his mouth and throat had become infected with abscesses, and he needed an operation on his throat. His parents were allowed to visit him. At the age of three, he was staying with his aunt and cousins (Robert and his elder sister Eliza) and they were playing nurses and patients in front of the fire. Eliza was the nurse and they were the patients. His aunt came in to take a pan of boiling water off the fire, Eliza bumped into her and the boiling water spilled over him. He put his hands up to shield his face but his arms were badly scalded. He was rushed to hospital and had to spend some weeks there. His parents were not allowed much access. He remembers they once brought him some little toys and after they had left the Sister took them off him, following a struggle, as she wanted him to go to sleep but he wanted to cuddle them. He never saw them again. He sat back, sighed and then said, "But all in all I had a happy childhood." Illness and loss both trigger the attachment system, so it was significant that the earliest associations he brought to me were memories relating to childhood illness and accidents.

When I left their house after this first session I thought, "He has lost the use of his legs, he has lost his grandson. What does he expect of me? What can I do? How can I help?" Then I thought of a quote by the French philosopher, Simone Weil, whose whole life was marked by an exceptional compassion for the suffering of others. She said, "Those who are unhappy have no need for anything in this world but people capable of giving them their attention. The capacity to give one's attention to a sufferer is a very rare and difficult thing. It is almost a miracle; it is a miracle" (Weil, 2009). This gave me some hope and some guidance on how to proceed. During the following week I was lucky enough to come upon another quote, this time by Peter Lomas (2000) who talks about a psychotherapist and says, "... her capacity, from everything she has learnt in life, to understand in her heart the experience of the other person and to respond with wisdom, compassion, intelligence and honesty." Fortified by these two memorable quotes I arrived for our second session.

Again I found Alfred sitting in his chair facing the garden.

Janet sat nearby and I remembered that she too had suffered the terrible loss of their grandson and the trauma of Alfred's stroke, and was now his main carer. This was another unusual aspect of the therapy. Although I was there to see Alfred, Janet sat in on almost every session and as the weeks went by, she joined in more, offered more information and asked questions and generally participated in the therapy. I was there for therapy with Alfred but at the same time I knew that I was also there to help Janet. Alfred told me that the next day would be his 85th birthday and I asked how he was going to spend it. He replied that his children would be visiting and they would have a birthday tea. I asked him about past birthdays and he immediately began to speak of Michael and how he used to love having him and his other grandchildren around him. He was particularly close to all of his eldest daughter's children, as he and Janet had looked after each of them in turn from the age of six months until they started school; later on, they would often have them after school and during the school holidays. They had been very hands-on grandparents, so he had strong memories of Michael as a baby and small child.

Alfred told me that Michael's older brother, John, suffered from Asperger's Syndrome. I wondered about the impact this may have had on Michael growing up and whether he had learnt to suppress his own feelings for fear of burdening his parents even more. Alfred told me that Michael had always been a gentle and sensitive child, a worrier and a perfectionist, always aware of hidden dangers.

I have long known that the skills of a psychotherapist are sometimes akin to those of a detective; seeking out clues as to hidden motives, behaviours and underlying resentments. Except in this case I was trying to understand the reasons behind a young man's suicide through the filter of his grandfather's perspective, in order to help that grandfather to understand his grandson better. There were many layers to peel back. This was another reason why the therapy was somewhat unusual. Forming a narrative is an essential part of relational psychotherapy so that an understanding is reached and made sense of, in order that acceptance and mourning can be made possible as part of the grieving process.

During our third session Alfred described to me the terrible day on which they learned of Michael's suicide. Michael and his younger brother had been at home while their parents had gone on holiday with their oldest son for a few days. James woke up early one morning to discover that Michael was no longer in the house, had left no note and had given no indication where he was. James telephoned his parents, who began to travel home, and he rang his grandparents who drove over to him. After a few hours had passed with no word from Michael, they phoned the police and local hospitals. During this time Alfred recalled that he prayed earnestly for Michael's safe return although he was not normally a religious man. Eventually they received a call from a local hospital to say that a young man of Michael's description had been brought in. He was dead on arrival. On leaving that session, Janet stopped me before I walked out of the front door to tell me that Alfred did not actually know the way in which Michael had died. To spare him from knowing the worst they told him that Michael had taken an overdose, had been found unconscious and taken to hospital but could not be revived. In fact, he had jumped in front a train. She asked me if I thought it was wrong to keep the whole truth from him. They felt it might prompt another stroke if he knew what really happened. I replied that I would think about it and discuss it with her the following week.

I discussed this first with my supervisor because it did present a dilemma. However, we decided that it was kinder to let Alfred believe the story his family had told him, at least for the moment. The next week I told Janet this when she let me in and she seemed relieved. This dilemma remained unresolved, as I continued to feel it would not be in Alfred's best interests to tell him the unvarnished truth. It was bad enough that his grandson had killed himself. Did he really have to know how?

Alfred said he just could not believe that Michael had intended to kill himself. He thought that perhaps his grandson had been trying to self-medicate and it had all gone wrong. Apparently Michael suffered from Irritable Bowel Syndrome (IBS) and this depressed him considerably. Alfred told me that Michael's birth had been very traumatic and he had great difficulty in feeding; so much so, that by the age of six months Michael was severely underweight and his mother was distraught. They had managed to resolve this by changing his milk but he always had digestive problems and Alfred said that these seemed to run in the family. Alfred had suffered from duodenal ulcers in the past and their youngest daughter also had a mild form of IBS but coped well with it. I thought of Michael's older brother suffering from Asperger's and felt there might be some familial link. Alfred then told me that for a couple of years before Michael's death he had been cutting his arms, which had shocked them all greatly. His mother took him to their GP who said it was just "a phase" and he would grow out of it. I felt angry when I heard this, as it was clearly a cry for help on Michael's part, a definite indication that he was deeply troubled, but it had been completely dismissed. I was beginning to get a feel for Michael. I also wondered if the doctor *had* taken the cutting seriously and organised appropriate treatment, then perhaps this young man might still be alive ...

Alfred told me more about his family. Their son and second daughter were both unmarried and shared a home together, the house that previously belonged to Alfred's mother. His other two daughters were both married and each had two children. Alfred said that when their oldest daughter was getting married it was rather a fraught time, as their future son-in-law kept calling off the wedding and she would come home in floods of tears. This happened about three times and they were getting increasingly anxious and upset with him. However, the wedding eventually went ahead but not as it had been planned. They married quickly and quietly. Alfred said their son-in-law, who is of a Mediterranean background, did not want much to do with them; for years, their daughter would visit them without him, even once she had the children, so they rarely saw their son-in-law. Their son-in-law was a quick-tempered man and their daughter did not have an easy time of it with him; their oldest grandson had once said to them, "Dad isn't a bad man but why does he have to shout so much?" Alfred said that Michael's death had completely devastated his father and he was a changed man. He now visited them occasionally and even helped them out in many ways, such as fixing a ramp outside their front door so that Alfred's wheelchair could be pushed up and down. Alfred said that he was now getting to know his son-in-law.

Michael had been at university but after a year decided to take a break and had been living at home doing various odd jobs. Apparently he was reserved but quite popular, although Janet felt that he did not socialise very much. Alfred said that Michael loved to debate – he and James would often argue about the "big issues in life" and he liked to discuss things with Alfred. He said that, as children, they often took them on nature walks and on walking holidays. He and Janet liked to go on holidays in the UK, usually in rented cottages, where they could go out rambling all day. Losing the ability to walk was a great sadness for Alfred, although he practised regularly and told me he could manage to walk the length of the room with the aid of a stick. His ambition was to be able to walk in the garden again.

I reminded Alfred about what he told me previously and asked him if he might like to continue telling me the story of his life. He said he left school at 16 and at first was apprenticed as a draughtsman at a society that made Ordnance Survey maps. However, he was not that accurate at the work and they sacked him after three months. He said he had not liked it there that much anyway. His father found him a job in a large company, initially as a clerk, but they trained him and he eventually became a technician. He stayed there for the rest of his working life and this was where he met Janet. He said it was a very good company to work for. When he was 18, in 1944, he was called up for National Service; for some reason he was assigned to a Scottish regiment and was sent for training near Edinburgh. He recalled one night exercise where they were supposed to dig a slit trench, but it was freezing cold and after a few inches of turf the ground was rock solid and none of them could dig it. At night, they had to lie on groundsheets using their waterproof capes as a kind of tent and it was unbearably cold. Hot lentil soup was distributed and he said it was the best meal he had ever had, because it warmed him through. In 1945, although the war had ended in Europe, it was still going on in the Far East and he was sent to Singapore where he stayed until the end of 1946. When he returned he was sent back to Scotland and contracted dysentery, as did many other men, due to dirty water. They were all so ill that the army could not cope and sent many of them to civilian hospitals. He was sent to Kilmarnock where he stayed for three weeks. He was very weak when he was discharged and was put on light duties for some time. He was demobbed at the beginning of 1948 and, fortunately, his previous company took him back.

In 1949 he attended a works dance and met Janet. However, they only started going out together properly in 1951, as he was too shy to ask her out. Within a short time he knew he wanted to marry her. He was 26 and she was 21. They became engaged and had to wait 15 months before getting married as they had to save a bit. They both lived at home with their parents, neither of whom had room for a newly married couple; Alfred and Janet did not want to live with their parents anyway. They found two furnished rooms which was where they started their married life. They married sooner than their parents wanted – their parents hoped to see a big white wedding but Alfred and Janet did not want to wait so long. Janet wore a blue dress, which her sister made, and it upset a few people. Her aunt had wanted to make a wedding dress for her. At first they were both so sexually inexperienced that things did not work out very well but their landlady was very kind and sympathetic; she advised Janet to attend a Family Planning Clinic, which she did, and they were extremely helpful and informative.

The following week Janet told me that, since I had been coming to see them, Alfred had been less withdrawn. Apparently, for quite a while beforehand, he had been so quiet that he sometimes did not speak all day; also, he never said a word to the carers who came night and morning to help with washing and dressing. When I went into the back room Alfred was immersed in a book propped up on his trolley. I asked what kind of literature he liked and he said that in the past he had always enjoyed reading technical books to do with his work, but had lately acquired a taste for mystery thrillers. He talked for a few minutes about his favourite authors and then lapsed into silence.

After some time, I mentioned that we had touched on some very painful areas the week before and asked how he felt about these things now. He said he would love to be able to ask Michael what had been troubling him. Personally he had a belief in the transmigration of souls, so he believed that Michael had now been re-born. He said he had read a lot of eastern philosophy and liked the idea of Karma.

At the next session Alfred was waiting in the living room as usual and smiled as I came in. I asked how his week had been and he looked at me with a twinkle in his eye before saying, after some hesitation, "Rather boring actually." Janet laughed and said he had visited the park one day and had been taken out by their son on another day, so it was less boring than usual. We sat quietly for a few minutes and I asked if had thought more about our session the previous week. He said he had and he felt it was better to talk through these things rather than holding it all in, as Michael had done. He said that Michael had clearly been troubled for some time as, although he had not noticed it, Janet had spotted Michael's depression but had not been able to draw him out on it. Janet intervened at this point and said she had been troubled by Michael for some time as she had noticed him becoming more silent and losing weight, and had also seen scars on his arms. During the winter his arms had been covered with long-sleeved jumpers, but in the warmer weather she had seen the scars – he had made no attempt to cover them.

The following week I asked Alfred how he was feeling; he paused for a time and then answered: "Helpless and a bit frustrated. Well, I am helpless really and there's nothing much I can do about it." We discussed his physiotherapy and how he could only go out when one of his children came to visit and could help to push his wheelchair. Janet was quite small and frail, so would have difficulty with the wheelchair on her own. He said he would like to be able to do more to help her. I commented that a nearby photo of him showed he used to be bigger and he agreed that he had lost weight. He said he did not like the food in hospital, so had lost weight during the two months he was there and had never put it back.

I asked how he had felt after our talking about Michael the week before and he replied: "I still can't accept that Michael took his own life – or even that he's dead. I know he's dead but somehow I still can't quite believe it." I commented that from all he had told me about Michael, I felt that he was quite a troubled young man and had actually been born into a family where there were a number of difficulties from the outset. Alfred looked at me for a long time and then said, "Yes, there were some difficulties; John, for one thing. He wasn't always easy to live with but Michael took a very protective role. He was more concerned about safety than John was. I remember one occasion when they were both small and we visited a wildlife park. We drove through the monkey enclosure and the monkeys were jumping all over the car and pulling at things. Michael became quite upset and told his mother to drive quickly to get out of there as soon as possible, but John wasn't bothered at all." I said I felt that maybe Michael had learned from an early age to hide his own feelings so as not to cause any further upset to his parents. Alfred thought about this and said, "Maybe you're right there. He didn't let on to anyone how he was feeling."

Alfred told me that Michael had been put on anti-depressants but stopped taking them of his own accord, abruptly, without weaning himself off them, as he felt they were not helping him. I thought that was unfortunate and someone should have picked up on it, but it seemed that Michael had fallen through a "gap in the system". Alfred said Michael had many friends, unlike John who always had trouble making friends and was "a loner". He said that luckily James seemed much more grounded, although he was unable to come to the funeral as he was too upset. He said he remembered, after the funeral, John said to him, "Maybe Michael has found some peace now" and I commented that was a sensitive remark from someone who might not always have been able to understand how others felt.

Alfred told me that he was also taking anti-depressants because the hospital staff thought he was depressed, but he was not so sure that they were helping him. However, he continued to take them. I asked him if seeing me was useful to him and he said, "Oh, yes, it's very helpful." Janet confirmed this to me as I was leaving.

The next week Alfred seemed more cheerful – his sister Clara was visiting from America, and she and her husband had been to see him. They had brought a large bottle of whiskey but, unfortunately, he could no longer drink that due to his medication. He told me that his brother-in-law was a geologist and that they both enjoyed hiking, so they often went on walking holidays, even though they were no longer young. He said that the stroke had also affected his swallowing, so he needed to have all his food mashed up; he also drank a supplement because his weight went so low.

We talked of how Michael had a lot to carry – what with John's Asperger's, his father's volatile temper and tendency to shout a lot, and his own IBS and depression, which had caused him to cut himself. Alfred had once heard Michael say that he thought he would never be able to hold down a job, because of his IBS, and that he would never be able to marry and have children. Alfred did not know why his grandson thought that way and we agreed that Michael might have been helped if he had had someone to talk to about all his problems. He clearly did not want to burden his family with them. Alfred remembered when Michael was still quite young and they had taken him and John to something which involved some street entertainers, Punch & Judy or something like that. John had happily walked towards them and wanted to join in, but Michael became quite frantic as he thought

John was putting himself in danger. He thought that Michael was always very sensitive, perhaps too sensitive for his own good.

Alfred fell silent for a while until I asked him what he would like to talk about. He replied that he was not sure but he liked to remember holidays they had been on when he was younger and was able to do things – he now felt frustrated to be unable to do very much. His walking was improving but it was very slow-going; also his left hand, which was curled up on his chest, was painful. Although he did try to exercise his hand, it was not showing much sign of getting better – however, it was not as painful as it used to be. I asked about his holidays and he said they used to go on walking trips to Dorset, Dartmoor and the Isle of Wight. Their son had particularly enjoyed walking and still did. Neither his son nor his youngest daughter had ever married, and she was particularly shy. On holiday, the family would always share a house together and self-cater, because she was too shy to share with someone else; she had never had a boyfriend, as far as they knew. He said that their second daughter was the most outgoing of them all; she and her partner had two children but had always refused to get married – which made Alfred laugh. When she became pregnant, he had asked if she would marry her partner, but she saw no need.

At the next session Alfred said he was pretty much as other weeks and we talked about his depression. He told me, "the doctor thinks I'm depressed so just gives me anti-depressants. I don't know if they're really working that well and I don't like the taste of them because they start to dissolve in my mouth and they're very bitter." We discussed how it was only natural for him to feel very sad about Michael, but that was not necessarily the same as being clinically depressed; both he and Janet agreed with that. Janet added that was the reason they had requested therapy for Alfred, so that in time he could possibly come off the anti-depressants. They both thought he needed to talk things through with someone. The GP only wanted to increase his dosage but Janet would not allow it and insisted on getting therapeutic help instead – to which the doctor agreed. I commented that it was not really possible to medicate a deep psychic wound; Janet nodded and said "exactly".

Alfred talked about various incidents in the past involving Michael; these demonstrated his grandson's caring nature and the fact that he had tried to protect John, who had seemed unaware of physical danger much of the time. We spoke of how John's Asperger's Syndrome would have made him less aware of certain things than most people and how Michael seemed to take it on himself to take care of John. I commented that he seemed to take all the family's troubles on his shoulders and this had obviously proved too heavy a burden. Alfred nodded and said that might explain some of it.

The next week Alfred spoke about his love of penguins. He became quite animated as he told me about how penguins live – he seemed very knowledgeable about them. We went on to talk about dolphins and elephants and how these animals all seem to have a kind of community spirit; they look after their families and care about them.

He then went on to tell me how he and Janet had taken out savings policies for each of their grandsons when they were born, to mature when they reached 21. Sadly, Michael had died one month after his 21st birthday and Alfred spoke of all the wasted potential, apart from the enormous distress to everyone. He said again how he hoped Michael has been re-born into a happier life. We discussed his own mortality and how he thought he had a duty to stay alive for as long as possible. He did not believe we can be sent to heaven or hell based on just one experience of life. He felt that we need to have quite a number of lives in order to grow spiritually.

At our next session, I asked Alfred what kind of a week it had been and he replied, "Oh, nothing special." There was a long pause and then Janet reminded him that he did want to ask me about something, and he nodded. He said he was a bit upset because he and Janet could no longer sleep together in the same bed. After his stroke they had moved a hospital bed into the front room and that was where he slept. There was no room for another bed in there, so Janet still slept upstairs in their double bed. He said at first it had not mattered so much but now they both missed each other at night; it made him feel lonely and miserable, not even being able to cuddle each other. I suggested they could install a chair lift to enable him to get upstairs; Janet said that at first he would not have been able to get on and off one, but his strength had improved over the months and perhaps now he could manoeuvre himself on and off a chair. However, the cost had put them off. I said that maybe they could enlist the help of their GP as I felt that, under the circumstances, Alfred might be eligible for some financial help for this purpose. Janet said she would see what she could do and she laughed that it was contravening his human rights – to which I agreed.

The following week she told me she had not got anywhere with the stair lift, as she had been sent from pillar to post when she telephoned the council. I offered to help and duly rang them when I arrived home. A few weeks later, Janet said there had been a visit from a council officer who came to see their house and took some measurements. However, they had decided that even if a stair lift was fitted, Alfred probably would not be able to get on and off it safely enough, so nothing was done. Nevertheless, the council representative did suggest fitting a better ramp outside the house, which was duly completed some weeks later, and they were both very happy about this.

Several weeks later, we had a session where Alfred spoke more about John, their oldest grandson. He remembered back to when John was small, before he was diagnosed with Asperger's Syndrome. That had been when John was about eight years old, but they remembered he had been somewhat strange before that, behaving rather obsessively and fixating on certain things, such as electric fans, which fascinated him. He never seemed to make friends at school and needed extra help in the classroom. He also suffered from a mild form of epilepsy and he talked about how electrical circuits in his brain seemed to have gone awry. Alfred said that, when John was in his late teens, he became quite violent and particularly recalled one incident when he threw milk bottles at his father after a row and the neighbours called the police. He and Janet went over there and the police came, and it was decided John should return home with his grandparents. He stayed with them for about two weeks and Alfred said he did not seem at all remorseful for what he had done, but Alfred persuaded him to apologise to his father.

The next week, Alfred was sitting facing the window with his book open in front of him. It looked as though he had read most of it. I asked him if he was enjoying it and he said, "Yes, it's quite exciting in places." I commented that he had read it very quickly as he only started it last week and he said, "it takes me out of myself." I asked what kind of a week it had been and he said it had been quite difficult because his cough was still bad. Sometimes he experienced a fit of coughing that left him purple-faced and gasping for breath, however the doctors did not seem particularly interested or worried about this. He wondered whether the coughing was something to do with the stroke. Alfred continued that when he was in hospital, he feared that he might be sent on to a nursing home or care home for the rest of his life, as he did not think Janet would be able to look after him at home. Tears came into his eyes and he said, "But then Janet said she would be able to cope and they brought me home and moved my bed down to the front room; she organised carers to come in and get me ready in the mornings and evenings and she *has* coped." He paused and looked at Janet. She smiled at him and for a moment their love seemed to fill the entire room.

After a few minutes Alfred declared, "But now I have to come to terms with Michael's death. I know he's dead. I know he's buried but I still find it so hard to accept that he killed himself. I feel it must have been an accident even though they tell me it was suicide." We spoke more about Michael's ability to hide his depression from everybody, his cutting and how that had been a cry for help that went unheeded. If he had been given the chance to unload some of his feelings, then he might perhaps have grown to feel less despair about life and that it might have been worth living.

The next session took place in the week before Christmas and the house was very festive with a Christmas tree, fairy lights and red tinsel draped round the bookcase and the mirror. Alfred seemed happy and started reminiscing about past Christmases, and then spoke of some of his army experiences. He told a story of finding a cobra in a bag of tools when in India and how they all stood in a semi-circle round it until one man tore a branch from a tree outside and stunned the snake with it, and then another chopped its head off with a machete. He also spoke of how he used to enjoy adventure books about exploring far-off lands, as long as they had a pretty woman featured in them. He laughed and said that "boy's own" stuff with just adventures and derring-do did not have as much appeal – he liked a bit of romance as well. I had lent him the book *The Girl With The Dragon Tattoo* and he had finished it and said he found it "quite exciting in parts" and very readable; I promised to bring him the second part next time I came.

After a pause I asked how he was feeling regarding Michael and whether talking about it over the last few months had helped him. He sat quietly for some time and then said, "Yes, it has helped. I wasn't really talking about it at all before but I was thinking about him every day. In fact, I was thinking about him most of the time and I still do think about him a lot but I know I have to accept it because he's gone. I know he's dead but I still can't believe he meant to kill himself. He had so much to live for but didn't seem to realize it. I think he felt he had a huge disability because of his IBS and he was trying to self-medicate for that and it went wrong." We all sat silently for a few minutes and then Alfred started to discuss their plans for Christmas and who was coming over.

At the next session, after a few minutes talking about his health, Alfred said he was still finding it very hard to believe that his grandson had intended to commit suicide. I replied that, as Michael had been suffering from depression at the time, then he was probably not behaving rationally and might have acted in a way that was quite unlike his usual behaviour. Alfred said he must have been a very good actor as no one realized how much he was suffering, not even the professionals; he added that Michael's mother had taken him to see a psychiatrist and a clinical psychologist in the months leading up to his suicide. I said I hadn't known that before and therefore she must have appreciated that he was in need of help, and Alfred confirmed that was true. She told them afterwards that she knew Michael was unhappy but not to the degree that he must have been. However, neither of the professionals had been able to help him as they only prescribed medication. There had been no suggestion that talking to a therapist might have been able to help, and Alfred questioned whether he would have opened up to anyone anyway. We discussed the possibility that Michael had been rejected by a girlfriend, and that this may have contributed further to his depression. Janet added that he had recently failed his driving test for the fourth time and that this might have been the final straw for him, "the last nail in the coffin" as she put it.

We agreed how tragic it was that Michael had felt he had no one to talk to about his own feelings, and Alfred said he felt guilty that his grandson was unable to confide in either him or Janet. We decided that his father had probably felt the greatest burden of guilt after Michael died, as he was the one whose behaviour had changed the most and who had seemed to be most affected by it. Michael's mother had seemed to be much stronger and, although desperately sad, she had kept herself busy and appeared to be getting on with life. I said that Alfred had no need to feel guilty, as he and Janet had given Michael so many happy memories and had always been good grandparents to him. Alfred nodded and replied that Michael had given them many happy memories too.

Our next session was quite taken up with talking about care costs and how his savings had dwindled due to the economic situation; Alfred and Janet had been told that they could only keep £6,000. I questioned this and suggested asking their son to investigate as I thought the amount was much higher.

Alfred informed me that he was practising his walking and it was getting stronger; he hoped to be able to walk in the garden by the summer, although he still had to use a stick and needed someone to stand nearby in case he lost his balance.

Alfred had almost finished the last *Dragon Tattoo* book and said he had enjoyed reading them. I asked how he had been and he replied that it had been an "up-and-down" week. He had to go to hospital for a check-up and was kept there for 11 hours with no offer of food. Fortunately his son had taken him, so he went and bought something to eat. Alfred was exhausted by the time they returned home again.

At the following session Alfred said that John came to visit them over the weekend and he seemed to be making good progress. He was doing some work as a dog walker, which he really enjoyed as he loved dogs. He had also settled into sheltered accommodation and wanted them to visit him there, so they were planning to go the next weekend. He said that John has always had his passions for various things – ranging from insects to fast cars and boats, and now dogs. These fads usually lasted for a couple of years and he learned a huge amount about them, and then moved on to something else. He said that James was doing well at university but missed Michael dreadfully and had agreed to have some counselling there; Alfred and Janet both thought that this would do him good. They would not get to see him until he came home for the next holiday. Alfred went on to talk about the book he was reading and spoke of various films he had enjoyed about historical events, such as the original *Titanic* film and *Zulu*, which he said was one of his favourites. He had read about Rourke's Drift and thought they showed it very well in the film, and he liked Michael Caine. He also liked the film *Apollo 13* and found that very absorbing.

The following week Alfred told me a lot about various books he had read regarding philosophy and different religions, and said he liked the ideas they conveyed. He reiterated his belief that he thinks it is only right we have a few "attempts" at this life, so we have a chance to live life well at least once and then maybe move on to a higher plane. At the end of the session Janet said she was pleased that he had "opened up" so well and that he seemed to be quite animated, as sometimes he could sit for hours and not say a word. She said he really looked forward to me coming so that he could talk about things that interest him. On my way home, I realized this had been the first week where we had not spoken about Michael at all.

At our next session, Alfred was sitting and reading when I arrived. I asked how he had been and he replied, "Up and down." He said he was thinking about Michael a great deal and was feeling sad much of the time, but he denied being permanently depressed. We discussed Michael for a while, and how his clinical depression had probably led him to thinking his life was worthless and that he would be better off out of it, without considering how this might affect the rest of his family. I said how stopping his medication so abruptly was a tragic mistake; Alfred felt that someone in authority should have told Michael of the dangers of doing that, so he would have known to wean himself off it gradually. We went on to have a philosophical discussion about Alfred's views regarding life, death, mortality, what happens to us before and after we are born, and how living a good life will probably elevate us to some higher plane in the next life. He said there really only needed to be two commandments; the first would be to love your God and the second to love your neighbour as yourself. At the end of this session, Janet said how pleased she was that Alfred had a chance to talk on this level, as otherwise his days were quite monotonous; and so our sessions stimulated him. I felt it was an essential part of the work with Alfred to discuss books, religion and philosophy as it opened up a "transitional space" for him, as discussed by Winnicott (1953). This was the clinical meaning of what I was attempting to do with Alfred.

At the following session, Alfred said he had decided that Michael must have been a perfectionist and perhaps could not live up to his own expectations. He asked me why some people think so differently from others and I said that was a huge question. He said his one comfort is the fact that he believes the soul goes on after death. This led him to talking about Dianetics and a book he'd read about this. He spent a long time explaining this to me and it seemed to be about the conscious brain and the subconscious brain and how traumas can be reprocessed using the subconscious brain and I said it sounded like the EMDR treatment (see Note 1 at the end of Chapter 1), which I explained to him. At the end of our session he thanked me for a very interesting discussion and we wished each other a good week.

Alfred was reading his book as usual when I arrived for the next session. When I asked about his week, he said he had been quite busy and had been taken out a couple of times, once to gardens with a lake at the centre. He had enjoyed that greatly, sitting and watching the ducks and swans during the warm afternoon. He spoke of outings he used to take with the family and then told me about his experiences in hospital immediately after his stroke. He explained that the stroke had been caused by high blood pressure rather than a blood clot, which meant he had a better long-term outcome. No brain cells had died as a result, although his left side had been seriously weakened. However, he was doing his exercises regularly and hoped to regain more strength as time went on. He then continued to tell me about Michael and I asked if he felt he was learning to cope a little better with the situation. He replied that, although it was always going to be painful for him, he felt that the weeks we had spent discussing it had really been helpful. He had a strong belief that Michael's soul had been reincarnated, which made him feel better. He also spoke about John's Asperger's condition and Michael's IBS, and we discussed the possible connections. Janet asked if Alfred's reaction to Michael's suicide was a form of post-traumatic stress disorder (PTSD) and I said I thought it could be described as that, but that his talking about it had released a great deal of his grief. Janet felt that Alfred had been much easier regarding it over recent weeks and appeared to have reached a certain acceptance. I asked if they would still like me to visit and they both responded positively; Alfred added that he looked forward to my visits.

The following week, Alfred was finishing reading *The Day of the Jackal* and put it to one side when I arrived. I asked how his week had been and he said, "good and bad." When I enquired further, he began to tell me a story of how they had won a Premium Bond prize, so I congratulated him, but Janet explained that it actually happened years ago when the children were still quite small. She reminded Alfred of this and he said, "So, it was last century?" and she said, "yes"; he laughed and said his memory was not what it was.

Alfred spoke again about his belief in reincarnation and I asked if he felt that he might meet Michael again once he has died. He was not sure about that and thought it depended on whether or not he had another life to live. He launched into one of his deep philosophical discussions about how people get to live different lives according to the one they have just lived. This led to him talking about the nature of good and evil and how some people respond well to life events while others do not, and how some make good even if they have made a bad start to life. We also spoke about how people deal with their anger and he said he felt more sorrow than anger. At the end I commented again that he had many wonderful memories of Michael and he agreed that was true but it still felt like such a waste that his grandson had never managed to achieve his potential. I agreed that this was the tragedy and that none of us expect to outlive our children and, more especially, our grandchildren.

Alfred had almost finished *Fair Stood The Wind for France*, which I had lent him a couple of weeks earlier, and said he was enjoying it although it had taken a while to get into it. He then had an alarming coughing fit, which Janet dealt with very calmly and efficiently. Once he was over that and was sipping a drink, he became very quiet; Janet continued that it had been quite a good week and they had visited a new park which they both enjoyed. However, Mother's Day was somewhat subdued as, although they had been visited by two of her sisters and their husbands, which Alfred enjoyed very much, that date would also have been Michael's birthday – so this was on everyone's mind. She said the next month would be much worse though, as it was the anniversary of Michael's suicide. She spoke for some time about her family, how Alfred got on so well with them all and how Michael's death had shocked them all so much. Alfred was sitting very quietly, so I asked him what he was thinking about. After a long pause, he answered with a smile, "young ladies", and then went on to say that he thought the opposite sex was a natural thing to think about sometimes. I commented that I thought he had been rather a shy young man and he said, "I still am"; we had a chat about how women used to scare him slightly but how he liked Janet's personality as soon as they met. This led to a discussion about women's changing role in society and how different things were when he was young; and he felt that things had become much better for women and he admired the way women had more say in their lives these days. At the same time, he said he did not always like the way they dress; he thought his grand-daughter, who was 18, had very short hair and trousers and so looked more like a boy. He had preferred it when she was younger and looked more feminine, with long hair and pretty dresses.

Alfred was reading as usual when I arrived for the next session. Janet told me that she had become increasingly worried about him during the week as he had been so quiet and withdrawn, and their children had also commented on it. Therefore, she had been to see their doctor and explained Alfred's state; she asked whether perhaps his medication could be reduced. However, the doctor advised that she could not discuss her husband's medical condition due to patient confidentiality. Janet had felt very annoyed at this, as she had organised everything for Alfred, sat in on all his medical appointments and kept the doctors informed. However, she had arranged for a doctor to visit him so that he could speak for himself. I asked Alfred why he felt he was withdrawing and he said that his coughing fits frightened him; he thought they may be exacerbated due to speaking, so he had become rather silent in order to avoid having them. I said that was a reasonable explanation but that speaking did not actually affect the coughing fits, which seemed to happen randomly and appeared to be unconnected with him talking. He nodded and did begin to speak more freely after that.

Alfred went over Michael's suicide again and said that he was starting to come to terms with it. He realised that Michael had been much more depressed than any of them ever knew; he only wished Michael could have felt able to share his despair with them and possibly they could have averted such a tragedy. He also reminded me that, on the morning Michael disappeared, he had prayed very hard for his grandson's return and that he would be found safe and well. However, his faith in prayer had now been damaged as the prayer did not work. We talked about this and how one person praying, however sincerely, may not be as powerful as a number of people praying. I also commented that Michael may already have died by the time Alfred started praying, which would have meant his prayers could not possibly work; Alfred said he had not thought of that. This led to Alfred embarking on one of his discourses about faith and he spoke for some time about his personal beliefs. These included his belief that angels are extra-terrestrials of some kind, as they have been mentioned by so many people going back to biblical times. He thought there was a strong possibility that we are not alone in the universe and felt there must be life elsewhere, and that we are just a small part of a much larger structure.

I mentioned that it had been nearly two years since Michael died and he looked surprised and said, "Has it been two years?" Janet confirmed that it had and Alfred said it still felt like yesterday. I thought that showed how deeply affected he had been by Michael's suicide and he nodded. For the first time since seeing Alfred, he started to cry and said how he simply could not understand how Michael could have done such a thing. "Didn't he realise the pain it would cause us?" he asked. He said he had spoken to James the other week and had asked him if he could ever do what Michael did; James had replied, "No, because I've seen what distress it causes to those left behind."

By the end of our session, Alfred seemed much more responsive and alert; he was talking about enjoying the sunshine, maybe sitting out in the garden, and perhaps being able to go out during the week to a park or somewhere. We also discussed Michael's funeral, which he had not been able to attend, but said how Michael was buried in a beautiful cemetery on a hilltop. He spoke about how it was just Michael's "envelope" buried there and his essence was elsewhere. He hoped that Michael was now living a happier life in another body.

I felt there had been a parallel process going on whereby Alfred had been mourning his own illness, mortality and "lost potential", and part of his own mourning had been projected on to the loss of his grandson. Michael had so much to live for, but all his potential had been wasted and taken away. In a similar manner, many of Alfred's reasons for living had been taken away, but at least he had become more animated and some of his vitality had returned.

We are all engaged in a constant flow of past and present, future and beyond, death and afterlife and reincarnation, taking us back again to the past and the present. Alfred was nearing the end of his days on this earth and was trying to bear the pain of losing someone who was so dear to him, and in whom he had invested so much love, hope and expectation. He had had many of his dreams shattered and during our time together I tried to help him come to terms with the loss of those dreams and those expectations. It was not easy and Alfred's pain was palpable but I believe that therapy allowed him to express and feel his anguish, an anguish that otherwise he would have had to keep locked inside himself. He gained the ability to express and share his pain with another and thereby lessen it.

# Chapter 6

# "I'm someone with a future and not just a past"

Training to become an attachment-based psychotherapist naturally concentrated my mind on my own attachments and I realised many things about my parents that I had not seen clearly before. I had known for a long time why my mother could not be the hands-on mum I would have preferred but I began to understand more about her and about our relationship. She was the oldest of eight children and had done more than her fair share of childcare while she was still a child herself. As the oldest, she had been held responsible for setting an example to her younger siblings and that was an onerous duty. She was often punished if one of her younger brothers or sisters misbehaved because her father said that she set them an example – therefore, she had to be perfect! She also wanted to help her mother as much as possible, so was doing housework and looking after young children from an early age. No wonder she did not want to take on more of the same as an adult and so became a career woman. She did not really have much choice in the matter, as she had to go back to work when Frances was three months old, having just been widowed. She again had to resume working when I was three months old, due to financial necessity, so Frances and I were both brought up by other people from infancy onwards.

As a young woman, my mother was a dress designer and worked for a successful fashion house, but she gave that up on her first marriage. After marrying my father they went into business together, starting their own dress factory. Thereafter her life was non-stop work as she was both the creative director and the driving force of their business. Life at home was not much easier, despite the help of au pair girls and a cleaning lady who came three times a week. Her working day was long and hard, and then she would return home late and begin cooking. There were no freezers in those days and no ready-meals − not that either she or my father would have countenanced them. I learnt from an early age that women were constantly busy and also that they were the ones "in charge". Although she was not around much during the week I had a strong, if somewhat ambivalent, attachment to my mother. I always knew that she loved me deeply and did her best to be a good mother, particularly during my difficult teenage years. I always felt close to her, even more so after having children myself.

When I started my psychotherapy work, I was initially shocked at how poorly some children were looked after by their mothers and how some young people received virtually no love at all. One of these was Faith.

# Faith

Faith's start in life was not auspicious. She was born prematurely to a young mother who already had a one-year-old daughter and was married to a violent, alcoholic criminal 23 years older than her. Faith spent her first weeks of life in a hospital incubator. At the age of four months she and her older sister, Justine, were taken into care and their father was sent to prison. Initially, she was fostered and then given back into the care of her mother. On her father's release from prison, when Faith was three-and-a-half, he once again began to terrorise his family. Her mother abandoned the two little girls and fled, having first shot her husband with a stolen gun, badly injuring his hand. The girls were again taken into care and Faith spent her childhood and adolescence living in 27 different homes with intermittent visits home to her father. He intimidated the social workers so much that they allowed him to take his girls, even though this was clearly not in their best interests and was against the advice of a clinical psychologist – who had said they should never be left alone with him. Faith attended 18 different schools, the last being an establishment for "delinquents" in the East End of London, because the local authority had nowhere else to send her.

When Faith first came to see me she was 45 but looked about 30, a tall, slim woman with long brown hair, attractive features and an air of wariness and edginess about her. She seemed weary of life. She told me she felt suicidal most of the time and could not understand why she had ever been born "into this crappy life". She felt angry, bitter and resentful at what life had given her so far. After a few sessions she brought with her a large dossier, which she had requested from the Social Services some years previously. It detailed her early life, although the first seven years were missing due to a fire at the offices where her records were kept. This dossier made for utterly depressing reading. Faith informed me that some of the things written there were untrue. For instance, when she was aged eight and at a girls' boarding school with her sister, the headmistress found Justine's behaviour too challenging and decided she was a bad influence on Faith, so thought it best to separate them. Faith remembers the parting as being very distressing and clinging to her sister, begging to be allowed to go with her. However, the report said that Faith had requested to stay at the boarding school. She told me that their father had taught them to be as difficult and disruptive as possible, kicking social workers on the shins and so on, and always asking to be sent home to him, telling everyone how much they missed their father. In fact, Faith was terrified of her father but was too terrified to do anything other than follow his instructions.

Her father would come and visit them whenever he could and would demand that they return home to him for visits. Sometimes he did not deliver them back on time or would not open the door to the social workers. On other occasions, he made the girls hide and refuse to come out, so they would not be seen, or he would move home and the Social Services would lose track of them. On one occasion, when Faith was six, neighbours complained about screaming from their house and the police were called. When they arrived they discovered Faith with two black eyes and covered in bruises. This time she was made a ward of court. Faith described how her father insisted that the girls were top of their classes at school and he maintained this by constantly drilling them at home. Unfortunately, Faith was dyslexic which made learning difficult for her. She recalled hours of standing in her bedroom trying to remember spellings, while her father would question her and hit her with a skipping rope whenever she answered incorrectly. She remembered these times of utter terror, wishing that she could die. He also liked his daughters to be dressed beautifully so that he could show them off to his friends in the pub. He told them he was grooming them to become prostitutes at the age of 16, so that he could live off their earnings; she and her sister were subjected to sexual abuse by him and his friends from an early age. She was taught to do whatever he or his friends wanted, and she had painful memories of this abuse. He would also take nude photographs of his daughters, some of which she brought to show me. She felt uncomfortable about the photos, even though they were taken when she was so young.

Faith said that she never felt happy as a child and would cause a lot of trouble wherever she was living. She vividly recalls one incident from when she was ten and living in a boarding school. She often had tantrums, as a way of gaining attention, and one day she had a tantrum at dinner time – she let her tray fall to the floor, making an almighty crash. The headmaster arrived, led her out of the dining room and sat with her on the main stairs. He sat her on his lap and put his arms round her. At first she resisted this and struggled and kicked out, but eventually she collapsed into his arms and started to cry. He just cuddled her and she said, "That was the first time I realised what love was." Of course, headmasters cannot do this in today's politically correct climate but for Faith at that time it was a revelation and a turning point. It was the first time she could remember feeling that someone cared about her and was showing her how much they cared. This same headmaster used to allow her to come into his study and feed his dog, although she was not permitted to take the dog out. In fact, she herself was rarely allowed out. A pupil had to be in the good "green group" to go out and she was always in the bad "red group". However, she said she knew that the headmaster was trying to look after her as best he could, and she valued him and what he did for her.

A couple of years before this incident, when she was eight, her father had managed to arrange a home visit. He lived in a flat six floors up, that had an inner balcony overlooking a central courtyard. There was an argument about her not being expelled from school along with Justine, which he would have preferred, and he started to hit her and she fell over. He kicked her in the chest and she flew across the room and landed against the door. He opened the door, carried her out to the balcony and dangled her by her ankles over the courtyard, and told her that if she screamed or said anything he would drop her. She remained perfectly quiet but recalls the feeling of total fear. After a few minutes which seemed like an eternity he put her back on her feet. He told her to get out and she immediately fled down a set of stairs on the opposite side, knowing that he would follow her. She just ran and ran until she reached the main road and continued running until she eventually reached the home where she was living, arriving a day before she was due back. The staff in the home questioned her as to why she had arrived like that, but she would not say anything. She just remained mute and never told anyone about this incident until she related it to me.

She told me that she was always a skinny little girl, even though she would eat well and would often go for seconds at mealtimes. It was as though her body refused to allow her to thrive. Whenever she arrived in a new place she would work out pretty quickly who the children "in charge" were and she would ally herself with them as a form of protection. She said she often became a bully so as to avoid being bullied herself, and she would put on a hard exterior so that people thought she was a "tough nut". However, inside she always felt scared, worried and intensely sad. She could not understand why she had to endure such a miserable life, while other children had parents who loved them. She also told me she never had toys of her own – except for one Christmas, when she was given a toy typewriter, which she loved; the next year, it was put in the attic for safekeeping and she never saw it again.

There was a letter in her file from a psychologist, written when Faith was 12. It said, "A very lonely and depressed little girl: the problem is that her feelings of hopelessness and apathy are based on a very realistic appraisal of her life. She is aware of feeling acutely depressed at times. The danger of one's dealings with Faith is that she will tend to communicate her depression in a way which makes one feel impelled to *do* something in an attempt to cheer her up, interest her, etc., but this will only be experienced for what it is – a refusal to accept her condition so that she may actually feel more lonely. Only by allowing oneself to be affected by her attitude and sharing the hopelessness is she likely to be helped, but this will entail great anxiety for the adult in question." This letter and its wisdom greatly impressed me, so I allowed myself to be affected by her attitude and to share in her hopelessness, whilst also offering an alternative view of the world.

Due to the constant moving around and her disrupted education, Faith left school at 16 without any qualifications. At the same time she left care, was housed with her older sister in a flat and left to get on with life as best she could. She was totally unprepared for life, however. She had never acquired some of the most basic skills that people learn while growing up within a family. She did not know how to look after herself in the slightest. Sadly, her older sister's life had taken a fairly predictable turn. Justine had been very much her father's little girl and consequently had gone down the path he had mapped out for her. She was an alcoholic and drug addict, having had six children by three different fathers. Her oldest child was in prison, the middle three were in foster care and the youngest two were adopted soon after birth.

Faith could see the life her sister was getting into and she made a conscious decision not to follow the same path. This was despite being in a situation where that lifestyle could so easily have overtaken her. When she was 15, a man in a car used to wait outside her school and would speak to her. He said if she came with him he would take her to a wealthy gentleman who would give her a lot of money if she was "nice" to him. Faith knew what he meant and said, "No. If I did that, there would be no going back." I think this incident exemplifies her inner resilience and desire to master her own fate. As she was an attractive woman, she had no trouble finding boyfriends. In fact, they flocked around her, and her father had taught her well how to please men, but she had never really experienced a truly equal, or adult, relationship with a man.

Having no qualifications, Faith took whatever work she could find once she left school – and she had a strong desire to work – and quickly picked up skills through sheer observation and determination. She worked mainly in offices doing various admin jobs and in one job she became friendly with a woman, Claudette, a couple of years older than her, who took her under her wing and became her mentor. Claudette advised Faith that she would never get anywhere in life unless and until she obtained some qualifications, so Faith started studying and eventually applied to go to university where she studied Business and Marketing. It was incredibly difficult for her as, apart from being dyslexic, she had no idea how to structure an essay but her fellow students were helpful and with their assistance she eventually obtained a good degree. This did indeed open the door for her to better jobs and she worked her way up until she was an independent career woman, with a flat of her own, who drove a car and seemed to be in charge of her life.

Faith was helped along the way by various boyfriends; she became very selective about the men she went out with and chose older, richer men of a certain class who helped her out financially and gave her expensive presents. However, these boyfriends were also often manipulative and lacked understanding of her much deeper needs, which she kept well hidden. She never admitted to her upbringing and instead wove elaborate stories about her past, in order to cover up the many deficits in her life. She had cut all ties with her father when she was 21 and speculated to me that he had probably died since.

Her mother had eventually re-married and had another daughter, Melanie, when Faith was six, but she had no further relationship with her mother until she was eleven. She remembered buying her mother a cheap bracelet to wear for her wedding, but she never had the chance to give it to her as she was not invited to the wedding. Justine had eventually gone back to live with their mother, so Faith had occasionally tried to re-establish contact with her but had always been disappointed. Her mother once arranged to visit her at the boarding school where she lived and Faith waited patiently for her, but her mother never showed up. This happened more than once. It is easy to imagine the depths of despair this must have plunged Faith into, the sense of betrayal, abandonment and loss of trust. Faith grew up knowing that the only person she could ever really trust was Faith.

As an adult, Faith had little idea of what clothes to wear, how to behave in social situations and what was expected of her. She did not know how people spoke to each other in day-to-day situations because she had never really experienced "normal" family life, so had a tendency to speak her mind in a very blunt and forthright way, which often alienated people. She had no idea that she came over as rude or uncaring because she had never learnt the niceties of life, how to "soften the edges", how to be "civilised". She said she learnt everything she knew through observation, watching how people interacted with each other, spoke to each other, their body language and facial gestures. She was a baby in an adult's body.

When Faith reached the age of 40 she decided she wanted to see more of the world, so she embarked on three years of travel and went, on her own, to India, China, Australia, New Zealand, Thailand, Malaysia, Nepal, Indonesia and South America. She had built up some savings and her boyfriend at the time gave her extra money; she lived abroad very cheaply, often with the local people. Her travels certainly opened her eyes and her mind to many things and she learnt a great deal from the experience. She told me many stories about her travels.

During Faith's childhood, when she had been staying with her father, he would sometimes take her and Justine out on a Sunday morning. If they ever passed a church he would tell them that the people inside were just sheep and he would make bleating noises as they went past, making the girls laugh. So Faith grew up with the idea that religion was for people who could not think for themselves and just followed the flock. This was reinforced by the misery of her situation, from which she could see no way out, and she felt that God could never help her. However, when she went travelling she felt drawn towards eastern religions and the idea of karma resonated with her. The thought that maybe she was paying in this life for misdeeds in a past life allowed her to rationalise what had happened, which in turn enabled her to feel that maybe life was not so miserable and could in fact become better. This gave her some hope for her future.

On her return to London she resumed her life, but had a very traumatic experience about two years before embarking on therapy. She had been stalked by a man who lived near her. She had been friendly towards this man before he started to follow her and had even been out with him, but when she wanted to end their relationship he would not take "no" for an answer. One day, when she was out walking, he came beside her, stuck a knife into her side and forced her to walk with him. She was too frightened to call for help in case he used the knife on her and, after walking her to a nearby park where she thought he might kill her, he eventually marched her to his flat on an upper floor of a high-rise block. He kept her prisoner there for 39 hours, at knife-point, and threatened to throw her out of the window if she did not comply with his wishes. Eventually, she managed to persuade him to let her go to the bathroom, where she sent a text message to a girlfriend and shortly after that the police broke in and she was freed. She was in the process of taking him to court over this but was scared he might exact revenge on her once he got out of prison. She also felt she could not ruin his life forever by sending him to prison and letting him have that sentence on record, so at the last minute she let the case drop. The policewoman in charge of the case was horrified at her decision but Faith felt that she just could not condemn someone in that way and, after all, she had survived the ordeal.

However, she was totally traumatized by this event and for two months after it could not leave her flat. Eventually, she decided that unless she did something about this state of affairs she would be housebound for the rest of her life, so she forced herself to go out for a short time every day. Each day she stayed out for slightly longer until she was able to face the world again. I believe the way Faith handled this episode in her life showed her great strength and determination. Shortly after that, she was plagued by a number of physical symptoms, some due to various bugs she had picked up while abroad. She took herself to the Royal Homeopathic Hospital because her doctor had seemed unable to help with any of her physical complaints. The day she visited the hospital she saw six different physicians as the first one realised the complexity of her case. He referred her on to the psychology department where the specialists discussed the best way to treat her – that meeting led her onto the path of psychotherapy.

At our first session, I shared with Faith the story of an elderly acquaintance who had survived a concentration camp as a teenager. When the camp was liberated the soldiers distributed food and he was given a tin of peas. They opened it for him and he drank some of the liquid. It made him sick because it was too rich for his malnourished body. He had to eat those peas very slowly and very carefully. I likened this to the journey we were about to embark on, and Faith smiled and said she understood.

Faith described some of her early life to me and said that a doctor had once asked her to write down some of her feelings.

This had frightened her because she began to compose a fantasy of what she would do to her mother and half-sister: tie them up sitting opposite each other and mutilate them in front of each other, so that her mother would know how it felt for her as a child. She dared not continue to write any more, as she found this part of herself so scary.

One of Einstein's many memorable quotes is: "The intuitive mind is a sacred gift and the rational mind its faithful servant. We have created a society that honours the servant and has forgotten the gift." I approached this therapy by aiming to remember the gift rather than the servant and a lot of the work did indeed seem to take place at an intuitive level, "right brain to right brain".

When Faith arrived for her second session, I could see that she was very stressed and anxious. At my suggestion she had started to write up some more of her life, and when I asked how she had been doing she replied: "To tell the truth, it's been horrendous. When you asked me to write up about my life, I tried to start doing that but it completely paralysed me. It brought home to me how totally alone I am. No family, virtually no friends. In fact it just stopped me in my tracks and I couldn't move off the sofa. I couldn't get up to make myself something to eat. I couldn't even wash. I just sat, stupefied and frozen. If it wasn't for my friend who came round and helped me, I'd probably still be sitting there now. I really thought I wouldn't be able to make it here today. In fact, you must be aware that sometimes I won't be able to make it – and you need to be aware of how careful you have to be with me regarding suggestions." I said it had not been my intention to put her into such a state and she said, "I know that." I explained I had wanted to try and get some kind of coherent narrative of her life, but if it was all too much then she did not have to put herself through it – maybe it was too early, and she nodded.

During this session, Faith went on to tell me more of her various experiences in different schools, assessment centres and foster homes. She never made close friends, except for one boy she fell in love with, but they were later separated. She never kept in touch with any of the children she met and never stayed more than 18 months in any one place. At the same time her father was always "on her case" and kept trying to get his daughters back. "We were his pension plan," she said impassively. As she spoke about her father I felt a deep chill come over me, as though I was being frozen by an icy wind. I asked if she knew much about his background and she described a poverty-stricken childhood in Scotland. He was the youngest of ten children and his mother used to beat him every day because he wet the bed. They all slept on one big mattress in the living room and she would have to wash it daily because of him. His two oldest sisters became prostitutes and helped out financially as soon as they were old enough. She said she understood why he would have learnt that this was all women were useful for. However, she said there were also times when her father was quite kind to them and she actually felt more for him than for her mother, who had abandoned her without a thought.

Faith said she needed to be able to deal with her anger, which again was something that paralysed her and it was usually directed against herself. She said she hated herself and often thought about suicide. In fact, when she was 30, she did attempt to take her own life by hanging. At the last minute she stopped herself and thought, "What am I doing?" and managed to extricate herself from the belt she had tied round her neck. One of the reasons she had not attempted suicide again was because she had yet to make a will and did not want any of her family having access to her possessions. She really wanted to make a will, in order to know that her few things would go where she intended. We discussed how this anger was really directed towards her parents and all the other people who had let her down or damaged her in the past; however, she had managed to turn that anger inwards instead of towards those people. Faith is no longer filled with self-loathing. In fact, she values herself and does everything possible to nurture herself and look after herself as best she can. She has articulated her anger and has let some people know how she feels, and no longer allows anyone to walk over her or show disrespect.

I asked Faith what life had been like for her when she left "care" and she spoke about her relationships with various older boyfriends. One of these was married to an Italian woman who came from a Mafia family, although was not a criminal herself. This man friend helped her financially, housed her and gave her presents, including a car which he taught her to drive. However, she also described many scenes of arguments and strife. At one point she looked tearful and said, "I'm doomed, aren't I? I've never had any attachment to anyone, as a child nor as an adult, and I've read that someone with my kind of background is bound to suffer ill-health and die young." We discussed her physical ailments; her allergies, stomach problems, thyroid problems and skin problems. I said I thought there was a psychosomatic element, and that her conditions were probably a result of all the trauma and stress she had suffered. This aspect of our work together was significant and health issues took up much time. I had read a book about memory by Charles Fernyhough (2012) and quoted a passage to her: "PTSD sufferers can have difficulty in richly imagining their future lives, which fits with the growing evidence that remembering the past relies on similar mechanisms to imagining the future." She nodded thoughtfully and said she felt that was definitely true.

I asked Faith if she had ever had a mentor in her life and she told me about Claudette, who had persuaded her to go back into education. Faith had been on a government training scheme when she was 21 and had an interview at the end of it, where a woman asked what she would like to do. She said she wanted to be a social worker, and the woman was scathing and said, "You must be realistic – you'll never manage to do that. Think again." She felt completely undermined and was sent to another building where Claudette answered the door to her. She asked her what the matter was and Faith just burst into tears, at the thought that someone was acknowledging how she felt. Claudette took her into another room, made her tea and sat and talked to her, the first person in years to sit down with her and listen to her.

113

Claudette managed to get her some admin work in the same company, so that they worked together. They became good friends and, when Faith was made homeless, Claudette offered her the use of her room while she was abroad visiting her family. When Claudette returned, another girl left, so Faith was able to continue living there for a couple of years.

This friendship was pivotal in Faith's rehabilitation; it went a long way to restoring some self-esteem in her life and a belief that she could achieve things. It was Claudette who persuaded Faith to go back to studying, which led her to gaining a degree and, therefore, better work. It also opened her eyes to a different world, and she set her aspirations higher and began to think of what the future might hold for her. Claudette played a significant role in her life for about 12 years until she tragically died in a car accident.

Faith went on to tell me more about her mother and the terrible sense of abandonment she felt when her mother left before marrying for the second time, after which she did not see her again for six years. She often wondered why she felt so unloveable and decided it was because of the way her mother kept leaving her. She said she knew her father treated her terribly and she was terrified of him. However, at least he had always tried to keep her in his life, even if for very dubious reasons, and at times she actually felt some care from him. She said, "I have so many things to tell you, they are beginning to flood back to me now that I have started to talk, and I am glad I have somewhere safe to come and tell them."

At our next session, she said that telling me so much had opened up a lot for her. "It's not like ticking things off a shopping list," she commented. "I thought that telling you about them might just get rid of them but it doesn't work like that and I've been thinking about my childhood properly." She went on to relate that lots of other past events had started to come back to her and it was like each thing she told me triggered another memory, which in turn triggered a further memory and so it went on. It seemed to me that throughout her childhood she was like a shuttlecock being batted back and forth, with no say at all in where she was going. She said that was exactly what it felt like.

At around this time, Faith began to talk about her dreams and we started to look at these in depth; this helped us to gain a deeper understanding of what was going on in her mind at a subconscious level. For example, she told me about one dream involving her father, in which she shouted at him for abusing her. She next found a small package that she discovered was a valuable investment bond he had taken out for her. She ran away with the bond and was then hiding from him, as she knew he would be furious that she had found it. I interpreted this dream as allowing her anger against her father to come to the surface, but also acknowledging that amongst all the dross he had given her a tiny amount of good stuff. She sat back and said she thought that was very clever and made a lot of sense. She then described another dream which had involved her working in a large, impersonal warehouse where she lived with many other people, and there was a bed at the side of her computer. Everyone went to bed at the same time and at the end of the room a man of about her age appeared with a small boy. She beckoned the boy towards her and she took him into her bed and cuddled him. Next she invited the man to join them and they all finished up lying in the bed cuddling each other. She said it was not at all sexual, but just felt like one big family. I interpreted this dream as her accepting her masculine side, at first the child part of her and then the adult part, and being happy that they were all now united. She was very happy to accept this interpretation and said it made her feel so understood.

At one point I asked Faith about the lack of toys of her own in her life; at first she answered that she always had other children to play with and they would share the toys that were in the home. However, after a pause, she added, "I would have liked to own a teddy bear. They look nice." I asked what kind of a teddy bear she would have liked and she said a brown one with a bow tie. That week I happened to be in a Barnardo's shop and saw a brown teddy bear with a bow tie sitting on a shelf. I bought it for Faith and the next time she came I propped it up on a cushion on the couch next to where she sat. I explained I had bought it for her and she took it in her arms and cuddled it and gave a slow smile. This teddy bear became very important and over the next few weeks she added two more bears to her "teddy bear family". Some weeks later she said she was on her way home and went into a shop where she saw a lovely brown teddy bear, bigger than any of her others. She looked at him for a long time and then walked out of the shop telling herself she did not need another bear, and that the others would be jealous, but she felt very drawn to him, so went back. She picked him up and cuddled him and it felt so good that she bought him. He was wrapped in a bag and she went home feeling very excited and happy, and could not wait to get him home.

She introduced him to her other bears, lined them up and spoke to them all individually. She told them that she still loved them all and they were not to feel jealous of him, because she was listening to little Faith who really wanted this teddy. She said they all understood and each one spoke to her in turn telling her they were not jealous and they also loved her and only wanted her to be happy. She said that she did think of them individually; if she cuddled one, then she had to cuddle the others as well, so they would not feel left out; if she gave a teaspoon of food to one then she had to do the same to the others. She said she would not be able to relate this to anyone else as she knew she was grown-up now, but there was a deep need in her to do this and it helped her to deal with her own jealousy issues. I commented that the more we love the greater capacity we have to love and she smiled and said, "Oh, I like that idea."

These four bears were crucial in Faith finding her sense of self because she used to take them to bed with her, cuddle them and talk to them. In time, she told me that she had incorporated her five-year-old self into her adult self, then her seven-year-old self, her eleven-year-old self and finally her teenage self. This process took about a year and it was one she developed for herself by asking each teddy bear what might be wrong with the way she was feeling, and to explain what they needed at different times. She listened to the answers. One time they told her they wanted colouring books and crayons so she bought some and spent many happy hours colouring in, which she found soothing and absorbing, and said was something she had never actually done as a child. Another time, her seven-year-old self said she wanted more colourful clothes, so she went to a second-hand shop and bought herself some clothes which were red and yellow and multi-coloured, whereas for years she had worn dark blue or black or grey. She told me after some time that when I gave her the teddy bear I had not told her how to play with it, assuming she already knew that, but in fact she did not. She had to learn along the way. She said there were so many things that other people took for granted that she had never learnt, due to not being brought up in a loving family where these things would have come about naturally.

A consistent theme in the therapy, for a long time, was Faith's ongoing disputes with her upstairs neighbours regarding noise. This caused Faith intolerable stress and she eventually called the Council who sent a woman round to investigate. We spent many sessions discussing the noise problem and her neighbour who played loud music until the early hours. During the times when he was being particularly troublesome, Faith would always go downhill. It was as though her progress was very much two steps forward then one step back, and she would become depressed and unhappy and feel she was getting nowhere. Due to suffering from complex PTSD, she was hyper-vigilant anyway, so what might have been tolerable for other people was definitely intolerable for Faith.

One day when we were again discussing one of her bad nights due to the noise, she said she realised that his playing loud music was something that seriously disturbed her; she did not like it but she could not really understand why. I asked if she felt it triggered some bad childhood memories to do with music and after a few minutes she said, "Of course, it reminds me of when my father would play music and force me to dance in front of him – while I felt totally self-conscious, humiliated and fearful of being punished for being clumsy or not graceful enough. That also explains why I never feel right doing something I enjoy, as though I am going to be punished for it, because as a child I was never allowed to do anything noisy or messy. It was always, 'Be quiet, don't make so much noise, etc.' – it makes so much more sense now". We talked about the fact that the dancing was not a one-off event but happened throughout her childhood when she was with her father, so would have been reinforced in her mind as a horrible thing to be avoided if possible.

After this discussion, Faith felt better able to tolerate the noise because she had an explanation for why it upset her so much. At the same time, she took the decision to address the problem after many months of trying to placate and appease her neighbour. Once she had told the Council and also informed him what she really felt about his unsociable and unreasonable attitude, she felt released and empowered. She said she had never really fought back in any way before but now felt she had the right to state her own views and be taken seriously. In the past she had always thought she was the one at fault and needed to change, but now she saw that sometimes it could be the other person who was in the wrong. She said that being able to retaliate without fear was a new experience for her and one that she relished. "At last I can fight back," she said. This ability had taken her many years to acquire and her inability to do so in the past had severely damaged her self-esteem.

One of the biggest areas to tackle was Faith's relationships. When we first started working together, Faith said that she felt very lonely and isolated. She did not have any close friends, anyone she could just call up when she needed to talk about something or anyone she felt she could rely on who would care about her welfare. She went on to talk about friendships from the past and how she had always attracted troubled people. I explained how she would have veered towards people who gave her a feeling of familiarity, i.e. those whose lives had also left them traumatized, but perhaps now that she was changing herself so radically then her friendships would change too; Faith agreed that seemed to be the case. She said she now wanted to attract different kinds of people, those who were more assured in themselves and who would be mutually supportive and understanding about her past. However, she knew that she had often been less than open about her past for obvious reasons. She also had the view that she could not open up to people or ask them for help, as that would be showing weakness or make them feel that she was "sucking them dry" like a vampire. Using her own analogy, I said that she could look upon opening up to other people more as a kind of transfusion rather than a sucking dry; when you actually ask for people's help they are often willing to give it and do not regard it as a weakness on your part. They often then feel able to share more about themselves and in this way people become closer, get to know each other better and develop deeper relationships.

Faith said this was particularly difficult for her, as she had never spent long enough anywhere to develop such deep relationships and just did not know how to do it. Would she ever be stable enough to hold down a job and not have to carry a teddy bear with her, or always have to go and lie down quietly somewhere for a while to recover when triggered by something? She said her "emotional thermostat" was set so high, could she ever lower it sufficiently to live a normal life? I said I felt that if she could learn to regulate her emotions in everyday situations, as she had been doing by going shopping and interacting with people, then she would be able to extend that regulation to more triggering situations. Eventually she would indeed lower her "thermostat" and be more in control of how she felt and less at the mercy of outside events that other people appear to take in their stride. This seemed to placate her but it was a topic we constantly revisited as she negotiated the difficult journey through her various relationships that took numerous twists and turns during the course of the therapy.

It really helped Faith to read books about dealing with trauma, taking them to heart and following the exercises or advice that they gave. One of these books was *Waking the Tiger* by Peter Levine (1997), in which he describes a gazelle being chased by a cheetah. The gazelle has the choice of fleeing, which he cannot do as there is nowhere safe to flee to and would be outrun by the cheetah, or fight, which he cannot do as he is not strong enough to win against a cheetah, or freeze, which is his only viable option. So he "plays dead" in the hope that the cheetah will just go away, preferring a live catch. This was the option that Faith had often chosen, so had "frozen" and was therefore immobilized in a traumatized state. Peter Levine describes how, once the danger has passed, the gazelle can then get back on its feet, shake itself all over to disperse the frozen adrenalin state, so as to get itself back into a normal condition, and then move on. However, for a human being it is not so easy and they need to be able to practise how to get out of that frozen state. This was something Faith worked on by following the physical exercises Peter Levine described, and she began to incorporate those exercises into her daily life.

Another book she found helpful was *The Healing Code* by Alex Loyd and Ben Johnson (2011). This book helped turn around many long-held beliefs and enabled Faith to change her mind-set; it taught her techniques of forgiveness and understanding of her own reactions to events. The third book was *The Endorphin Effect* by William Bloom, and this seemed to have the most powerful effect of all; that could have been because she read it after absorbing the other two. She used the exercises in this book to help guide her through everyday traumas and problems, such as looking for her "strawberries", as William Bloom describes those incidents of pleasure that we all have. He also advocates giving yourself an "inner smile" and doing various exercises to enhance the production of endorphins. This is something that we can all do and incorporate into our daily routines until they become like second nature. There were times when she forgot to follow the advice given in these books and would lapse back into old ways of thinking and behaving, but once she returned to looking back at the books she was able to turn things round again.

As the therapy progressed, Faith became less tense and strained and was able to embrace happiness in a way that she had never experienced before. Her depression lifted and she no longer felt suicidal, although stressful events could still trigger her into old feelings of hurt, betrayal, anger and despair. However, she was now able to process these differently and understand them better. She made efforts to forge closer links with friends, those she thought would benefit her and with whom she could share some intimacy. One day, she said she felt a bit upset because she had texted various friends in an effort to make contact but they had ignored her messages. She asked me what she could do about that, as she really wanted to reach out to people and felt abandoned and rejected. I suggested that instead of sending a text message she might actually telephone someone to speak to them in person. There was a silence, before she asked, "Do you know how hard that is for me?" and I said I did understand how hard it was. However, at her next session she said she had done exactly as I had suggested and, to her surprise, had met with a positive response. Her friend had suggested meeting up and in fact they went to the cinema together, something Faith had not done for years. She enjoyed the film and invited her friend back for a meal afterwards.

After about a year of therapy, Faith decided she wanted to start reading some more, as her education was so lacking. She asked a friend to recommend some authors and her friend suggested Charles Dickens. Due to her dyslexia Faith decided to borrow talking books from the library instead of attempting to read them off the page. The first book she chose was *Bleak House* as, understandably, the name appealed to her. She started to listen to this work and found she loved it, especially because it is about orphans. She would talk about it in her sessions but a few days after she had finished it, she commented: "What a cop-out! He's such a great storyteller and then he goes and kills off one of the main characters instead of giving us a good back story. I've had it with Dickens!" However, this negative view did not last and over the next few months she read *A Tale of Two Cities, Nicholas*

*Nickleby* and other classics such as *Moll Flanders, Vanity Fair, Jane Eyre* and *The Vicar of Wakefield.* She said she particularly enjoyed Dickens' characters as she could recognize them from everyday life and could relate them to people she knew. She found the relationships described in books incredibly helpful to her in understanding relationships because the same rules applied in the present day as they did then. She derived enormous satisfaction and enjoyment from reading and I hope will continue to do so throughout her life.

Faith had some good business ideas which she wanted to develop, and her next ambition was to try and put these into practice by starting her own company. She had friends who could offer practical advice and she was beginning to take the first tentative steps towards turning her dreams into reality. Initially though, she was mainly concentrating on her relationships as she had become aware that relationships are of primary importance to health and well-being; so she was willing to put her commercial ideas on hold for the time being. In the past she was almost totally self-sufficient, because she had to be. There was no one she could rely on and no one she had ever been able to trust except herself; it had taken her a long time to be able to open up to other people and to allow her vulnerability to be seen. I think the most important aspect of this therapy was the building up of our relationship, which in turn I hope will allow her to establish warm relationships with other people.

Towards the end of the therapy, Faith joined two local classes – one for public speaking and the other for singing. These opened up her life even further and, although she was extremely nervous before the first public speaking session, she really came into her own and talked about her beliefs. She also met more people with whom she could connect and often went out with one or two of them after class. She said she could not sing at all but enjoyed the singing class. Both of these classes enabled her to "find her voice", as did talking to me on a regular basis.

I found Faith to be quite inspirational in her willingness to accept new ideas and take on board anything that would help in her quest to heal and rebuild her life, a life that could so easily have been destroyed by its terrible beginnings. Instead of letting that happen, she took charge of her own destiny and set about making her life worth living.

# Chapter 7

## Baking the cake

If people were cakes and you knew the ingredients that went into them, the quality and quantities, how they were mixed, at what temperature and for how long they were baked, you would have a fairly good idea of the end result. This might sound simplistic but I have generally found it to be true. Hearing stories of people's backgrounds, it is not difficult to see how and why the adult has turned out the way he or she has. I shall use myself as an example to show this and will then present several short illustrations based on people I have known.

I was a second child and my mother told me years later that she had experienced a miscarriage when I was three years old. This is an important fact because both my parents would have preferred a boy and it is possible that the miscarried baby *was* a boy, the boy they wished for but never had. As my father's only biological child, and another daughter, I was a slight disappointment to him. Although I did not understand this until I was much older, I did know that I could never really please him. He was a fastidious and pernickety man, a terrible worrier and nervous about many things, but he was also kind-hearted, hard-working and conscientious. He had an artistic side and a quirky, dry sense of humour. He was the sixth child in a family of seven; six boys and one girl. I wonder how much attention he received as a child and how much he was looked after by his only sister, who was two years older than him? He told me that it was his responsibility, from around the age of three or four, to look after his youngest brother and he continued to do so for the rest of his life, which may go some way to explaining his anxiety as an adult. They were the closest of all the siblings and his youngest brother could do no wrong in my father's eyes.

When my father met his future wife, he was in his early 30s and still lived at home with his mother. His own father had died when he was 14, and he and his siblings were therefore most solicitous towards their mother. She was a quiet and gentle lady who had come to England from Romania when she was about 11, in order to escape the pogroms. She was the daughter of farmers and had grown up learning how to milk cows and make butter and cheese. She rode horses and used to swim in the local river and skate on it in winter. She was an excellent cook and, despite not being able to read or write, could cook and bake elaborate recipes which she obviously carried in her head and had learnt through observation. My father would visit his mother every Friday on his way home from work and would invariably return home with a freshly baked cake for the weekend. I believe I learned how to cook from observing her when I stayed with her as a child. Her method of cooking scrambled eggs is still one I use today and is different from any recipes I have ever seen.

My father became an embroiderer. Soon after the war, he was asked by a friend to see a lady who needed some embroidery work. She had designed a dress that featured two embroidered Scottie dogs on the collar. That lady was my future mother and so my parents met. Fairly soon my father also met Frances, who at that time was about five years old. Following a year of courting he asked my mother to marry him by suggesting she might like Frances to have a younger brother or sister. He was a good-looking man and many of his mother's friends had their eye on him for one of their daughters, but he had not been out with many girls. He was too fussy and rather shy and felt intimidated by anyone who seemed too pushy. He also did not like "flashy" girls and was greatly put off by too much make-up or revealing clothes. Both of my parents were quite Puritan in their outlook. Meeting my mother through work was the perfect way for them to get to know each other without either feeling pressured in any way.

Once they married they went into business together. My

mother had worked as a dress designer for various fashion houses and so decided they should start their own dress factory. They asked one of my father's brothers to join them. They worked incredibly hard to build up their business and the house was always littered with sketches my mother had drawn. When she was younger she had regularly gone window shopping and would come home and adapt some of the designs she had seen, incorporating her original ideas into them. Once she had made some sample dresses, she enlisted one of her sisters to take the samples to the big stores to see if they might be interested and this was how she began to get orders. She had "made a name for herself" by the time they went into business together.

During school holidays I would often stay with one of my many relatives for a few days or maybe a week at a time. If there was nowhere to send me, then my parents took me with them to work; I would sit in the little office adjacent to their workroom with a book, drawing paper and crayons, amusing myself for the whole day. Sometimes, I would go into the main workroom and watch dresses being made. I soon learned that my mother was the one in charge.

Staying with different relatives throughout my childhood showed me that not all families run along the same lines. I learned to be adaptable. I was also on "best behaviour" most of the time, as I did not want to "show my parents up" in any way, so I was polite, obedient and malleable, fitting in wherever I was put. It was a relief to be at home but even there I could rarely "be myself" as I was not supposed to cause any trouble to whichever au pair girl was there at the time. When we had our family holiday in the summer, I relished having some proper time to spend with my parents. I remember my happiest moments, talking to my mother about books I had just read or sitting near her, while drawing or playing quietly. Just being close to her was sufficient.

There were many times when my mother could not be there, such as when I went for an interview for the girls' grammar school I later attended. She was too busy at work to accompany me, so my father took me to the interview instead. I was the only girl sitting in the waiting room with her father. It may be more common nowadays but I felt a little different because of this. There were times of loneliness too and many evenings waiting for my parents to come home, but having to go to bed before seeing them. I would force myself to stay awake, to make sure I could have a few words with my mother when she came to kiss me goodnight.

So, looking at the ingredients and the way they were put together and the manner in which they were "baked", what might one expect? It is hard to be purely objective about oneself but I think I turned out fairly predictably. I learnt to observe others from babyhood onwards, always on the lookout for the slightest nuance of a person's mood and how he or she might act. I felt inhibited in some ways, unable to express myself freely, and it was only when I met my future husband that I felt relaxed enough with another person to "be myself".

In fact, I did become engaged to someone else some years before meeting my husband. I was young and inexperienced, and this man used a good deal of emotional blackmail to ensure that I felt responsible for him. I became engaged under pressure on his part and, because I thought that not many other men would be interested in me, I went along with it. We were engaged for six months before I summoned up the courage to tell him that I felt it would not work. Those six months had let me see him in his "true colours" and I knew that if I allowed the marriage to take place then it would be a disaster. He took my decision very badly and I felt riven with guilt about the rejection I had put him through. However, I knew I could not marry him. It was a decision I never regretted.

Once I felt more secure with the help of my husband, who gave me what is known as "earned security", it enabled me to follow my own dreams and ambitions in life. One of these was to give back some of the help and support I had received over the years from people whose empathy and compassion had impressed me. This led me onto the path of exploring ways to help others.

Motherhood had also given me a certain confidence, so when the opportunity arose to study attachment-based psychoanalytic psychotherapy, I felt ready to do the necessary work. I had been employed as a personal assistant/secretary before marriage, and once the boys were settled in school, I worked part-time in various jobs. During my training I volunteered as a Samaritan, as I thought my newly-found knowledge would be of value in listening to people, and so it proved to be. My sister, Frances, died two weeks after I had qualified. She had suffered from early-onset Alzheimer's for 13 years, since the date of diagnosis, and for several years before that.

One maxim I have always adhered to, as a therapist, is that I am no better or worse than any of the people I see. We are all human, and the people who come to see me are going through particular problems in their lives. They have come to seek my help because they feel I have had the training and experience to provide that. It does not mean that I am in any way better than them. Some clinicians take a superior attitude, which I think is a mistake. We are all trying to negotiate this life in the best way we can. Some people inherit particularly difficult family legacies and do need help before they can live their lives in a better way. I would like to describe some of those who have sought help because the "hands they were dealt" were really hard ones to "play".

# Veronica

One of these people was Veronica. She was referred to me by a colleague who was treating her husband. To any outsider, their life might have seemed ideal. They were an affluent couple, lived in a lovely house, had two sons, an enviable lifestyle including two or three holidays each year, and Veronica was a very attractive woman; blonde, blue-eyed, slim, beautifully dressed.

She was in her late 50s when she first came to see me and had been seeking help for her overwhelming anxiety for many years. This had come to the fore in recent years, when she finally felt able to express her anger about the way her husband behaved towards her, particularly sexually. She had been treated with cognitive behavioural therapy (CBT) which can do little to help deep-rooted problems, as it is a rational approach to over-whelming emotions absorbed since birth. During our first session, I asked Veronica to tell me about her childhood. She hesitated and said that no one had previously asked her about that. This was despite years of visiting different therapists. Some had even suggested that talking about the past was not helpful.

The story she told me explained so much. Her father was a Holocaust survivor, who had been put on the Kindertransport as a young teenager by his mother, to whom he waved goodbye and never saw again. He made a life for himself in England and became very successful in business, in fact, becoming a millionaire. However, due to the pain of losing his mother in the way he had, he vowed never to become emotionally close to anyone ever again. This applied to his four children, of whom Veronica was the third. Her mother was his first wife and she too had come from a traumatic childhood in Germany. After she had their first two children, she had an affair and they separated for a while, but he then took her back and she went on to have two more children with him. Subsequently, she had another affair and they divorced. Veronica was nine years old at the time and remembered sitting in the back of a car waving goodbye to her mother, who she only saw again during the summer holidays when she and her siblings went to stay with her. Her father employed a nanny and a housekeeper to look after them. He went on to marry twice more. Her mother married five times.

Veronica told me that she could never remember her mother playing with her. She recalled asking if they could play together, but her mother would always be reading a book and would say, "When I've finished reading." However, on finishing one book, she would immediately start another one. Her oldest sister became her surrogate mother. Once their parents were divorced, Veronica's life was split between a rigid and regimented routine at home, run by Nanny and the housekeeper, and a totally laissez-faire household when staying with her mother in the summer holidays. She allowed them free rein and Veronica recalls smoking, drinking and attending parties when she was 14, and even being encouraged by her mother to sleep with her boyfriend. These two extremes left her in a kind of limbo, never having a "secure base" with either of them.

Throughout her adolescence, Veronica found the way to attract her father's attention was by being ill, so she played up genuine complaints in order to garner as much attention from him as possible. Her health problems were genuine, but she exaggerated them and spent time in hospital and had various operations, culminating in a hysterectomy when she was 22. No one appears to have explained to her the ramifications of such an operation, apart from saying that it would help her gynaecological problems. She was not offered any kind of psychological support and it was as though her physical problems had been dealt with, so that was that.

She married young, at 19, fairly predictably to a controlling man. While she was in hospital having her major operation, her husband was with another woman. She divorced him soon after, and began to make a different life for herself, starting a business which became successful. By the time she was in her 30s, she had her own home and was running her own business. She had several relationships, but felt that most of the men she fell in love with did not want to marry her, because she could not have children – until she met her present husband. He was younger than her by a few years and had come from a totally different upbringing, more conventional and much less wealthy. He found her to be a breath of fresh air, after the younger women he had been dating, and he did not mind that she could no longer have children, saying that they could always adopt.

They married and did, indeed, adopt two boys two years apart. Veronica tried to be the best wife and mother she could, but with little example of how to do that. She followed her Nanny's regime of strict routine and expected her sons to behave in the way she wanted them to. She was creative and did many projects with them, allowing them to be messy and get dirty and play as children should; however, she was also very controlling and often shouted at them, so there were lots of arguments in the household. At the same time, she only really felt needed and validated through sex, and wanted her husband to make love to her as often as possible, to prove to herself that she was loveable. He, in turn, liked her to dress up in sexy lingerie and generally "perform" for him, not realising that women had their own needs. Lovemaking was all about pleasing him. She often told him that this made her feel like a prostitute, but he did not seem to understand. She put up with this situation because her fear of rejection and abandonment was so great that she would have done anything to keep her husband. After about twenty years she rebelled and demanded to be allowed to "join in" their sex life instead of just being used. They went to see a sex therapist and for a short while things improved. Unfortunately, her husband then had health and business problems of his own, which caused him to go back to his default position of treating her as his sex object. He subsequently sought treatment for depression caused by his problems and soon afterwards she came to see me at his counsellor's suggestion.

During most of their marriage they had both used cocaine and marijuana to anaesthetise themselves against their own feelings, but had stopped using cocaine some months before seeking therapy. Veronica had been seeing other therapists throughout the marriage to try and help her cope with life. Exploring her childhood with me enabled her to see how the mixture of her upbringing, complicated by her parents' own backgrounds, had contributed to her internal struggles and the external expressions of those struggles.

The science of epigenetics tells us so much more now about how the effects of trauma on our parents or grandparents can still affect us today. In Veronica's case this goes a long way to explaining her need for control, set against her need for validation through the release and power of sex. This was the only area in her life in which she felt valued and worthwhile. In the rest of her life she had to exercise complete control over people and situations to make herself feel safe, to feel that nothing could unexpectedly shake the foundations which were already so shaky. At the same time she dreaded alienating people, in case she re-experienced the abandonment and rejection she had felt as a child. She also had to acknowledge the impact a hysterectomy, at a young age and without any psychological support, had made on her life.

Once Veronica "rocked the boat", by questioning her husband's attitude, she found it impossible to go back to how she had been before. This led to tumultuous inner turmoil and caused an ongoing battle between them. Eventually, her husband began to take on board that their problems were not all due to Veronica, as he had led himself to believe. He started to question his resentment towards her change of behaviour and to take a look at himself. He began to accept that he might have a part to play in their marital difficulties and that his background had contributed to his own attitudes. Despite the many ups and downs they have been through, their love for each other remains and they are striving to make their marriage better.

I often think of therapy as unravelling the knotted threads of someone's life, helping them to undo the knots they come across, which can often be long and painstaking work, and then rewinding the thread so that they can continue more smoothly. Veronica's threads were so twisted and tangled that, although many knots have been worked on and some unknotted, there is still a great deal to be done. She is working through her many layers of buried pain and grief that manifest themselves in her anxiety and physical ailments.

# Rick

In contrast to Veronica, the ingredients that went into Rick's "cake" were very different. Rick came to see me after being persuaded to do so by his mother. He was in his late 50s, divorced and the father of three adult children, twin girls and a younger brother. I asked what was troubling him and he sighed and repeated my question, "What is troubling me?" After a pause, he said, "I think my main problem is with relationships." I asked him which relationships in particular and he said, "I've treated my mother disgracefully over the last few months, refusing to take her calls, never calling her, really worrying her. Also I don't have a good relationship with my children and one of my daughters is getting married next year and I can't even feel happy about it. In fact, I can't feel anything about anything much. I'm not in a relationship with a woman at the moment either, because I've finished the last three relationships I've had, each of which lasted about 18 months. I've been divorced for around eight years."

Rick was an only child and both of his parents were only children as well. His parents divorced when he was six and his father moved to America two years later. He used to phone Rick every two to three weeks, but Rick never really had much of a relationship with him. His father remarried an American woman, who worshipped him, but Rick felt that she had not always been treated very well. His father had been dead for about 13 years when Rick came to see me.

After the divorce, Rick's mother moved to a house next door to her parents. So Rick had quite a close relationship with his maternal grandparents, but it was a small family unit with no aunts, uncles or cousins. He did not particularly enjoy school, apart from sports, and left as soon as he could – at the age of 16.

He worked for various companies for a few years, but then started his own business and ran it from home. He much preferred to be in his own space and do everything himself.

Rick said that he was a shy child and did not have many friends. As a teenager, when he found his first girlfriend, he was also attracted by her family and therefore thought that she was "the one". They married when he was 20 and she was 18. It only lasted for three years before they divorced. He began to be more sociable and re-married at the age of 30. He said, sadly, that he felt he had been such a failure as a father. I suggested that he still had time to repair his relationships with all three of his children, particularly if he showed he was willing to listen to them and to learn from them. We looked at his early relationships and the kinds of blueprints he had been given for his future relationships. He said he had been a selfish father, spending more time seeing to his own needs than to his children's, and letting their mother do the major part of their upbringing. He said that, as he had worked from home, he used to take them and collect them from school, so felt entitled to play golf and watch football at weekends. However, he described family holidays and days out, all of which sounded normal and pleasant.

I asked why his second marriage ended in divorce and he said that after 20 years of marriage he just felt unhappy and wanted to end it. He could not say why this was. He instigated the divorce and they did it themselves without involving lawyers. He now lived in a flat on his own and said he was very happy there. He said, "At the moment I feel such a failure because I am relying on my mother. I'm 57 and I've had the big house and the nice cars and now I'm relying on hand-outs from my mother, who is 85. It's just not right." He could not understand why he had been treating his mother so badly, but said, "It's as though I'm taking everything out on her."

We had a discussion about being open and honest with our nearest and dearest, because he felt so ashamed of his behaviour in recent months. He could not feel happy for his daughter, who was engaged to be married, because he could not feel happy about anything. He had been on anti-depressants for some time but had recently come off them. His mother had been so worried about him that she called his doctor, who came to visit him at home unexpectedly and put him back onto them. He took the anti-depressants for two weeks but then stopped. I suggested he could call his daughter and actually tell her he felt ashamed of the way he had been behaving and would like to repair their relationship. He nodded and began to cry.

Rick described a solitary childhood, as his mother went back to work full time after the divorce, so he would come home from school and go next door to his grandparents; but when he was a bit older, he would stay at home alone. Not having siblings or cousins and with few friends, he had no experience of making deep bonds with people. He had no idea how to navigate the ebb and flow of intimate relationships. He told me he used to clean his room thoroughly at the age of 11 and have everything in its place, and thought this was usual behaviour. I said I felt it was quite unusual for an 11 year old boy to be so meticulous. He told me how he was very house-proud and liked to keep his flat perfectly clean and tidy. He described somewhat ritualistic ways of doing things, such as always showering when coming home after travelling by train into London, using wet wipes on the handle of a supermarket shopping trolley before using it, cleaning all tins before putting them in the cupboard and washing all eggs before putting them in the fridge. We looked at how this somewhat obsessive-compulsive disorder (OCD) behaviour was used as a way to make his immediate environment perfect for him – so that nothing could take him by surprise or "contaminate" him, and how this may have developed as an antidote to having no control over the events of his early childhood.

We also discussed Rick's relationships since his divorce and how they had all ended after about 18 months. I pointed out that his father had left when he was six and gone to America, events to which he had not attributed much importance. I suggested that he may have been influenced by them and been left feeling that one did not discuss awkward or distressing situations with people, but instead walked away from them, as his father had done. This was, more or less, what had happened in his marriage. The reasons why he had become unhappy in the marriage gradually emerged, but he had never discussed them fully with his wife. He had just retreated to another room in the house and led a virtually solitary life, even though he was still living with his family. Eventually, he could no longer tolerate that and so had instigated the divorce. This was how things appeared to be with his next three relationships. When things became difficult, instead of facing them and tackling them, he retreated into silence and sulking, the women became fed up and the relationships foundered.

A couple of months after starting therapy Rick embarked on a new relationship; after a short time, he decided that he was now okay and stopped coming for therapy. I knew that this was a mistake but had to wait until he realised this for himself. Sure enough, a few months later, he contacted me and said that things were not as rosy as he had thought they would be, and asked if he could resume the therapy; so he returned. He had fallen in love with the new woman and at first everything had seemed wonderful, but cracks soon appeared and old habits took over.

It was also getting nearer to his daughter's wedding. To his dismay, she did not want him to walk her down the aisle, saying that her uncle (his ex-wife's brother) would do so. He was devastated by this and was going to refuse the invitation to her wedding. I explained that, if he refused, then he would probably regret that for the rest of his life. I tried to show him how his daughter might be feeling about the situation, as he had virtually been out of her life from the age of 16 to 26. In the event, he went to the wedding with his new girlfriend, but did not participate in the way he would have wanted, and felt unhappy and somewhat bitter about it. Nevertheless, I pointed out to him that when he first came for therapy, he had been worried that he might not even be invited to the wedding and at least he had been there. He now had to build bridges so that the relationship between them could grow and flourish. He started this by inviting his daughter to have a meal with him once she was back from honeymoon. She came and he spoke openly to her about how much he regretted not being there for her for ten years and how he wanted to change that and be a part of her life again. She was receptive and acknowledged he had been a lovely father during her childhood, if a bit strict, but she valued that now and thought he had done his best for them all at the time.

Rick's relationship with his son had always been easier and that remained good. Things were more difficult with his other daughter and it took another couple of years before he could get on better with her. He explained to all his children that he was in therapy, and why; they were encouraging and praised him for the efforts he was making. I urged him to keep open the lines of communication and not retreat into his own world of solitude, shutting out everyone else. We referred to this as his "hedgehog" mode.

At the same time, Rick was not doing so well with his new girlfriend. At first everything had seemed fine, which was why he had initially stopped coming for therapy, but after a while she began to find some of his behaviour irritating and he felt under pressure to become someone he was not. He began to retreat and not communicate, and cut himself off from everyone for a while. He also threatened suicide and his girlfriend contacted me, but he refused to speak to me. Eventually, he did talk to me again and explained how desperate he felt when he realised that his new girlfriend was not quite the person he thought she was. Although their sex life was good, in other ways she was clearly dissatisfied. He felt he could never please her and that she was always bringing up past mistakes he had made and reminding him of them, whereas he wanted to move forward and start afresh. Despite having given her huge moral support while she was going through problems with one of her daughters, she finished the relationship due to her perception of his many faults and he once again fell into depression. He found it very hard to give her up and tried to win her back on a number of occasions. Although from time to time she appeared at his door and gave him some hope that things could be rekindled, ultimately she made it clear that she was no longer interested.

At this point we looked more carefully at Rick's past patterns of behaviour and he began to see how he had sabotaged relationships in the past. He started to look to the future and tried to make new relationships. He joined a dating agency and began seeing various women, some of whom he went out with for a short while, but no one really came up to his expectations. At the same time he was establishing a stronger bond with his married daughter and trying to do the same with her twin sister who was more difficult to reach. His relationship with his son had always been the easiest one for him and this continued without any problems.

Rick had men friends with whom he would go to sporting events and occasional social gatherings, and at one of these he met a woman who sparked his interest. He asked her out and they began to see each other on a regular basis. For the first time, he found someone he felt completely at ease with, someone he did not feel was judging him or trying to make him into a different kind of man. She was good company, he found her attractive and he described her as a lovely person. His married daughter became pregnant and the birth of his grandchild heralded a new chapter in his life. It brought him closer to everyone in the family as they all celebrated the new baby's arrival. He managed to revive the relationship with his other daughter until he felt that he had almost achieved a similar level of intimacy as he now had with his married daughter.

It was at this point we agreed that Rick could cut down on therapy, so initially he reduced to once a month, and after a few months he decided to have "one session per season" or four times a year. So far, this is working well and he is happy and content with his current relationship.

# Catherine

The final example of how our personal "cakes" can be baked is Catherine. She was born in Scotland, the younger daughter in a Jewish family, and she had one elder brother. He was "the blue-eyed boy" of the family and she knew from an early age that he was the favourite. There were certain expectations put upon Catherine to conform and behave as a dutiful daughter, to marry a nice Jewish boy and to become the ideal wife and mother. She was in her 60s when she came to see me and had already undertaken a great deal of therapy in her life, so I asked what it was she found most helpful about therapy. She thought about this for some time and eventually said, "I suppose it is being understood a little. Being allowed to talk and being listened to – knowing that I have a voice." This made a lot of sense because, as she described her early life, it became clear that she had been voiceless throughout her childhood and adolescence. She was a solitary child, always under the shadow of her elder brother who was clever and charismatic. He grew up to achieve great success in his chosen field.

I asked about Catherine's relationship with her mother and she said that she never received any love or affection from her mother and could never remember being kissed or cuddled by her. She said that some years before her mother died she had asked her about this; her mother had replied, "Oh, I used to look at you in the pram and think how sweet you were." She remembered her mother as devoting all her love to her elder brother. Her mother died, aged 97, and Catherine recalled saying to her brother, "I don't think our mother could ever express her love for us," to which he replied, "Oh, I didn't feel that. I always felt she loved me." Catherine felt that was probably true.

She felt much closer to her Aunty Sophie, her father's sister, who came to live with them when Catherine was 18 months old. Aunty Sophie was an Auschwitz survivor who had somehow managed to escape death. She had been sent to the gas chambers on three occasions; on the first, there had been too many people, so she was stopped from going in as the gas chamber was too full. On another occasion she hid up a chimney and avoided going, and on a third occasion a prison guard held her back and told her to leave. Apparently she was very beautiful and Catherine thought this may have helped her to survive. Aunty Sophie was in her early 30s when she came to live with them and it was the first time she and Catherine's mother had met. They also took in her father's brother for a while, after he had survived the war. Looking back, she sees this must have been difficult for her mother but at that time it was more accepted under the circumstances. Her father's mother and another sister had died in Auschwitz. He had come to England aged 18 to join his father, who had come here in the 30s to try to make a better life for them all. Sadly, he could not get his wife and his sister out in time. Her maternal grandfather had died when her mother was little and her grandmother had a great struggle to bring up her family, so Catherine understood that the niceties of parenting had passed them by. Life was just about surviving and fitting in, and not making waves.

Aunty Sophie lived with them throughout Catherine's childhood and she turned to her aunt rather than her mother, although she said she remembered her father being somewhat more affectionate towards her. She also recalled her mother saying she never really wanted more children after having her brother.

Catherine went to university, but, when she was 21 her father died while she was taking her finals and so she came home immediately after her exams. Unfortunately, her mother and Aunty Sophie fell out badly at this time and Catherine could not wait to leave home because of the terrible "atmosphere". She moved to London, where she shared a flat with a girlfriend. By the time she was 24 she felt "on the shelf", as most of her friends were married or engaged. Then she met Bernard and although she realised there was something a bit different about him, she also liked him for that very difference. In fact, he was on the Asperger's spectrum, something that was not diagnosed until years later. I commented that she had gone from a mother who could not show love or affection to a man who suffered a similar difficulty, and she agreed. She thought it was not going to work and suggested they split up, but a week later he came to meet her and asked her to marry him. She was so pleased that she accepted right away. They were both 25 when they married. Interestingly, she had veered towards someone who gave her a feeling of familiarity to the atmosphere she had grown up with, an absence of closeness and intimacy. She told me she feared intimacy, as it was something she had never known, so there was no danger of Bernard intruding into her inner world and disrupting it.

At first Catherine was the main breadwinner, as Bernard was articled to become a solicitor. She realised that many of his difficulties resulted from him being dyslexic, again something that was not diagnosed at the time. She very much wanted a child, although he wanted to wait a bit, but she became pregnant when she was 27. The pregnancy was not an easy one and she was taken into hospital early, as the baby was not growing properly, and she was induced. Although she was in labour for a long time, the baby showed no inclination to arrive; eventually she needed to have a Caesarean and baby Jessica was born weighing 4lbs. Catherine was totally exhausted and tried to breastfeed, under enormous pressure from everyone at the hospital, but found that she could not and so felt a complete failure. At home she had no help, as her mother was still in Scotland, her mother-in-law also lived miles away and she had no friends nearby. Jessica cried solidly for eight months. They lived in a townhouse and she remembers looking out of the first floor window, their living room, and feeling very sorry for any pregnant women passing by, thinking, "You don't know what you are letting yourself in for." We both decided she probably had post-natal depression but it was never diagnosed. She did go to see a doctor who just said, "Well, Jessica was a premature baby – what can you expect?" and she came out of the appointment crying. Bernard was working very hard, coming home late, so she tried to shield him from it all but often broke down in tears. When Jessica was eight months old, Catherine met her former boss who offered her a part-time position. She persuaded Bernard that they should have an au pair, to which he agreed, and she went back to work. She said her life began again. The au pair was very good and she felt extremely lucky.

The baby experience put Catherine off from having any more children but, when Jessica was three, Bernard suggested trying for another one as he did not want their daughter to be an only child. They moved to a larger house and she had Zoe just before Jessica turned four. Zoe was an easier baby and Catherine stayed home for 18 months, but then found another job working for the Social Services. The position was perfect for her, as it was only a ten minute drive away and she was allowed the whole of August off. On top of that, she loved the work. At about this time she and Bernard went for Marriage Guidance counselling and that was when she decided to train to become a counsellor. Up till then, her job had been responsible and interesting, and had also paid well, but she was constantly in terror that she would not be considered good enough or might be unable to cope. As a result, her life was filled with anxiety, although she loved her work and her team of colleagues. She had a terror of being "found out" and exposed as somehow not worthy enough.

We discussed how her upbringing had undermined her confidence in so many ways as she was looked upon as "just the daughter" – who needed to validate herself by being pretty and marrying well. I commented that she had always taken a back seat to everyone else in her life; she agreed with that and said she now knew no other way to behave. She actually found it strange to put her own needs first and considered herself to be selfish if she did so. During the early years of her marriage, once she understood the extent of her husband's own problems, she had tried hard to protect him and shield him from difficulties. This made me comment that she had also spent a lot of time "treading on eggshells". "Oh, all the time," she interrupted. "I have spent my life treading on eggshells."

Catherine also admitted how jealous she had felt of her brother's success, although not his fame. Nothing she had ever done had been looked upon as good enough, and her path certainly bore no resemblance to the glittering career her brother had forged. She said that Bernard had changed significantly over recent years and was now more willing to show some affection and appreciation, emotions he had such trouble expressing previously. However, she had spent so many years quelling down her feelings that she found it really hard to be in touch with them now, in particular anger or confrontation. She said that as a child, if she ever cried, her parents would say, "Stop crying or I'll give you something to cry about," and that feeling still remained with her. Her parents worked extremely hard to provide for their family, six days a week, and on Sundays would collapse at home utterly exhausted. Catherine learnt early on not to cause any trouble, be a bother of any kind or impose her own will in any way.

Both of Catherine's daughters were now married and she had five grandchildren, three of whom, Zoe's family, lived in the north of England. As Jessica lived nearer to her, Catherine had spent more hands-on time looking after her children than for Zoe. She had found it a delicate balance to reassure Zoe that she cared as much for her as for Jessica. Bernard's mother now lived in a care home nearby as well, so Catherine had many demands on her time. Also, Bernard suffered a few serious health problems while she was seeing me, which Catherine had to deal with, allaying his fears as well as managing her own. She said that in fact their marriage was in the happiest and healthiest state it had ever been, at this time.

Over the course of the therapy, which lasted for about 18 months, we explored Catherine's many doubts and fears regarding her responsibilities and capabilities as a wife, mother, grandmother, daughter-in-law, aunt, cousin, sister and friend, to the detriment of her sense of self and her place in the world. Over time, she gradually became more accepting of the person she was and how she had become that person, and was able to see why she worried so much about situations before they had even occurred; this gave her some peace of mind. Towards the end of the therapy Catherine decided that she did not want to leave altogether, as she knew she would still have episodes of almost "disappearing into a black hole". She felt that she would want to offload, so we agreed that, like Rick, she could come once a season, four times a year, and so far that has been working well.

I believe that these three examples show how the impact of people's early years affect them for the rest of their lives, setting up blueprints for how they will react and respond to other people and life events. If their sense of self is nurtured by love and sensitivity then they are much more likely to take what life throws at them and deal with it robustly. Sadly, there are many people whose parents cannot seem to provide unconditional love, mainly because they were not given that by their own parents, and so the patterns continue. Much of what is now considered to be genetic is actually the result of the environment in which a child is brought up, and whatever predispositions that child may have will either be ameliorated or intensified by their upbringing.

A simple example I would like to put forward is if one were to see a family walking by, where the father is obese, the mother is obese and their seven-year-old child is clearly overweight, would one think that was due to genetics or to the family's eating habits? Probably a combination of both, one might imagine. However, if that child had been taken from its parents at birth and brought up in a different family, whose eating habits were healthy and who believed in a lot of exercise, would that child still be overweight at the age of seven?

When I explored my sister's background and realised the extent of the disrupted attachments in her life and how many times she must have felt abandoned and rejected, is it any wonder that she had such difficulty in forming close relationships as an adult? By the age of eight, I believe my sister was probably deeply traumatised but no one seemed to recognise it. Her trauma was never dealt with and consequently as an adult her body showed the signs and symptoms of it, by developing an auto-immune disease, scleroderma; this was only diagnosed while she was having tests at the National Hospital for Neurology to establish if she had early-onset Alzheimer's. It is my belief that early life trauma predisposes some people towards developing dementia and if that trauma could be addressed while they are still young enough to benefit from help, then perhaps the explosion of dementia we are witnessing at the moment might diminish. Is it a coincidence that the people who were born during and shortly after the Second World War are the ones now developing dementia at a much greater rate than previously seen? Doctors say it is because of an ageing population that we are seeing more cases of dementia, but that does not account for those developing early-onset Alzheimer's, as my sister did.

There is much research done into the physiological causes of dementia, with so far few positive results, but little research is done into the psychological factors. For one exception, see White, Cotter and Leventhal (2018), who bring together a relational perspective into dementia origins and care. Separating the mind and body as Western doctors do, does everyone a disservice. People with mental health illnesses are treated differently from those with physical illnesses, which is nonsense. Just because you cannot see a mental illness in the same way as you can see a physical one, does not mean that it is not as real and debilitating. In the UK, people who suffer from Alzheimer's are expected to pay for their care, as it is deemed to be some kind of social problem instead of the illness that it is. If the root causes were tackled early enough, then maybe fewer people would go on to develop dementia, which is an illness that devastates so many lives – for the sufferer and all those closely connected with them.

# Chapter 8

## Granite man

In 2005 I attended the National Institute for Health and Care Excellence (NICE) Judicial Review regarding the prescription of Alzheimer's drugs, Aricept, Reminyl and Ebixa. I was there as a carer representative on behalf of the Alzheimer's Society. Speaker after speaker, including myself, told how these drugs can be helpful for people suffering from Alzheimer's, and the sooner patients are started on them, the better. The conclusion of the Judicial Review was that the drugs should not be prescribed in the early stages of the disease but only once the patient had deteriorated to a more severe state. It felt as though this decision had been reached even before the panel had heard any of the evidence – that came from doctors, neurologists, psychiatrists, nurses and carers. This was such a flawed and wrong decision that we were all stunned by it. The members of the Alzheimer's Society, who had attended the Review, went for a "debrief drink" afterwards and commiserated with each other at what a terrible decision had just been made. I said at the time that it would have to be reversed at some point as it was clearly the wrong judgement. So it turned out to be. The decision *was* reversed but not until four years later, by which time my sister had died.

In 2020 there is still no cure for Alzheimer's but Aricept is now routinely prescribed once a diagnosis has been made. The drug can help to stabilise some people at a higher cognitive level for longer, and the sooner it is prescribed the longer the effect can last. I had been fighting since 2000 to get Frances put on this medication but it was a wearisome battle. Eventually, after two years of pressure, her consultant at the National Hospital for

Neurology said that if we could find a private doctor to prescribe Aricept, then he would still monitor her on the NHS. I managed to do this but she had to pay for the drug privately. As she started taking Aricept when she was well into the disease, it only really worked for about twenty months but it did give her that extra amount of time during which she remained relatively stable.

My father died 21 months after we had all moved in together, at the age of 88. After his death we employed private carers for Frances, to come in for a few hours each week to provide a brief respite to my husband and myself. I was still working as a part-time doctors' receptionist and, although I enjoyed the work and the patients, I found the management and the doctors unsympathetic to my situation. I could not always leave work on time which meant I would not be home in time for when Frances returned from her Day Care Centre. This meant that we had to arrange for someone to cover for an extra hour or so each day. In fact, the carer we employed was earning more per hour than I was as an NHS receptionist.

After Frances had been living with us for three years, her condition had deteriorated to such an extent that her social worker advised it was no longer safe for her to continue living at home; so we should consider putting her into residential care. Frances had already fallen down the stairs once, breaking a toe, but that accident could have been far worse. She had also taken to wandering around the house without any clothes on, something that would have horrified her if she had known what she was doing. She was, by then, doubly incontinent and needed a great deal of help with everything. She would follow me all the time, shadowing me, as she did not like to be left on her own. It was a 24 hour commitment. As people have pointed out to me since, when a sufferer is in a care home there are three eight-hour shifts for the staff. When the same sufferer is living at home then the care is constant and usually falls on just one person.

My sons were both wonderfully helpful when they were at home and sometimes offered to look after Frances for the weekend in order to give me a mini-break. Their input was vital and also refreshing. They had a younger outlook and a different attitude. They would take it in turns to look after her in the evenings so that the other one could go out. I remember coming home after one weekend away and asking my elder son how the weekend had gone. He said a friend had invited him to go and play snooker with him on the Saturday evening, while my other son was out. I sympathised and asked what he had done instead. He looked surprised and said, "Oh, I went to play snooker." "What about Aunty?" I asked. He smiled and said, "I took her with us." Apparently she enjoyed herself watching the boys play and being included. I would never have thought of that solution.

My younger son used to take her out for coffee to places she knew and remembered, like Hampstead, where they would also go for a short walk. Frances had been such a kind and considerate aunt to the boys when they were still children. She had taken them out to concerts and the theatre, and introduced them to many of the pursuits she enjoyed, such as books, art and music. They fully understood how much she had deteriorated, even though many other members of my family did not quite believe she was so ill. They were unable to see the daily struggles or how she managed to create the illusion of being better than she was. Her vocabulary was so good that she could substitute other words when she forgot some, so was still able to maintain a conversation. In fact, she never completely lost the power of speech, even when she had lost almost everything else.

Although immediate family members were caring and supportive regarding Frances, and all of my friends and most of my cousins were sympathetic as well, other members of our large family were not always so understanding. This taught me how isolating and hurtful it can be, when those you would hope are closest to you actually disbelieve you and treat you as though you are somehow doing something wrong, when you are actually trying your utmost to do the right thing. This was an invaluable insight when it came to dealing with people who came to see me with their problems. I could have a glimmering of how it might feel for them to be misunderstood and not listened to, or have their own feelings unacknowledged, even though they were part of an ostensibly loving family. Sometimes though, with the best will in the world, therapy cannot undo the damage that has been wrought because the person is so sensitive that their wounds go too deep for effective healing. They become entrenched in their protective behaviours and unhelpful patterns, and too cynical to believe that a different way of behaving might be beneficial. One such person was James.

# James

James came to see me after a short course of couples counselling with his then girlfriend. The counsellor had recommended that he needed one-to-one psychotherapy and his girlfriend had agreed. He was a handsome man in his late 40s who had already received a considerable amount of therapy in his life, but had not found it of much use. He had a relatively high-profile job and was used to putting on an act in his public persona. In private, however, he was a totally different person. He described himself to me as extremely shy, depressed, morose, indecisive and not a nice person to know; yet underneath, he acknowledged that he was in fact a kind and caring person. He admitted to having made many mistakes in his life and therefore did not trust his own judgement. He said he always "self-sabotaged" and we looked at how his childhood had not helped him to achieve a solid sense of self. This had been exacerbated by the fact that when he displayed shyness, clinginess and need, he was met with ridicule and humiliation; resulting in him feeling constantly ashamed and therefore becoming deceitful in his relationships. He said his first girlfriends were never approved of, but rather than confront his parents and ask why this was, he just accepted that they did not like the girl. He therefore kept the relationship secret until he moved on to the next girlfriend – this pattern was repeated and reinforced throughout his life.

In his late teens James developed a passion for running and by the time he was in his 20s he found that the thinner he was then the faster he ran. So he began to restrict his food and ultimately developed anorexia. His family was worried about his weight loss but did not know what was wrong, until he eventually admitted to his girlfriend that he had anorexia and she managed to get him into hospital for treatment. It was quite a Victorian regime and he was the only man there. He stayed for three months being "fattened up", as he put it. After being discharged, he subsequently married his girlfriend. Although he knew at the time that this was not the right thing for him to do, he needed someone to look after him. They were married for two years, during which time they had a baby son. Shortly afterwards James had an affair, which he said was really a cry for help, a "get me out of this situation" plea. In fact, he felt he had been tricked into them having a baby, as it had not been planned. When his wife told him she was pregnant, his heart sank but he pretended that he was pleased, even though he felt unprepared. He told his wife about the affair and this led to them divorcing. The affair soon fizzled out and he began to live in digs in London and concentrate on his career. He saw his son regularly and was a dutiful, if distant, father. He said his relationship with his son, who was now twenty, was good.

James said his childhood was a happy one and he had not suffered any traumas. However, when we looked at it more carefully there were in fact many factors which, taken one by one and cumulatively, did actually represent an environment which was not conducive to him developing in an emotionally healthy way. He was the third child with an older sister and brother, each two years apart. Both of his parents were teachers and he always felt under pressure to perform well academically, but said he really had to work hard to achieve anything. They were a restrained family, never displaying emotions or talking about feelings. He never witnessed family arguments or dramas of any kind. Everything was very low key and they were quite insular, so the outside world seemed like a scary place. James learnt from an early age that anger, or indeed any strong emotion, was not tolerated so he repressed his rage; as an adult he often turned that anger towards himself, and so hated and despised who he was. The few times he turned his anger against other people, he felt terrible afterwards and spent most of his life trying to be the person he thought others expected him to be. He wore a professional mask much of the time, hiding his true feelings and his true self. He felt like an imposter living a life that was not actually his. No one knew who he really was. He recalled an incident in a previous therapy where the therapist sat silently, not responding to him at all. He felt so infuriated by this that he picked up a potted plant on the table and threw it at the window, shattering the glass. This ultimately ended that therapy.

He told me he used to wet the bed until he was ten, and although this was dealt with patiently and kindly, he still felt humiliated and embarrassed by it. His parents never sought any medical advice to establish if there was something physically wrong. He thought they would have been too ashamed to admit something like that to their family doctor, so they just waited until he grew out of it. I believe his anxiety about this just exacerbated the problem and caused him to continue wetting the bed. It may also have given him some extra attention, albeit of a negative kind.

James was a fussy eater, so mealtimes were strained with his parents "tutting" at his pickiness and refusal to eat certain things. This, again, caused him humiliation and embarrassment, and it is interesting that he later developed anorexia, as food and issues around eating obviously caused great anxiety. Anorexia almost always has as a contributing factor, or even as a main factor, the desire to remain as a child, with a child's body, and the subconscious wish not to accept responsibilities. James was also chronically shy and used to "hide behind his mother's skirts" metaphorically; this caused other family members such as aunts, uncles and cousins to tease him about his clinginess. Once again, he was subjected to humiliation and embarrassment. It was really no wonder that he grew up with feelings of shame and anger and difficulty in finding his own voice. He also had very low self-esteem and however successful he was in his career, in his personal life he felt he was an abject failure.

James recalled feeling happy with life when he was about five or six, but by the time he was in his teens this had evaporated and he lived with a pervasive feeling of doom and dread. This culminated in the depression he experienced throughout his adulthood, for which he could find no relief. He slept badly, as his work schedules involved night shifts and early morning starts. Every morning, he woke up dreading what the day might bring and he had to force himself to go to work, even though he was regarded as good at his job and in control of things. Deception actually ruled his life and he had to put on his professional "mask" in order to survive in his daily life. His life was about survival and coping rather than living with any enthusiasm or joie de vivre. He could not share any of his fears with colleagues, not wanting them to know what he was really like, and his shyness prevented him from communicating properly with others.

About 14 years before seeing me, James had a relationship with a woman who was the love of his life, although he was not sure whether he had ever really experienced true love. He knew Kate through work, which is where he met all of the women he befriended, as he was too shy to socialise and find girlfriends in other ways. He was stunned by her beauty and she made his heart leap. She was considerably younger than him and he felt he was "punching above his weight" when he actually plucked up the courage to ask her out. He was amazed that she accepted and kept thinking that she would someday find a younger man and leave him. They embarked on a relationship and lived together for about a year, but although his feelings for her were intense and passionate, they were never able to talk emotionally. This was something he was not used to doing and also, as usual, his parents did not really approve of her. In some respects, he and Kate lived parallel lives, not really connecting or communicating in the ways a couple normally would. Things would fester under the surface but neither of them would address any issues, as neither wanted to "rock the boat", and James had no experience of how to tackle emotional problems.

About a year into the relationship, James started an online conversation with a woman, which developed into a flirtation. Kate discovered this on his computer and they argued about it, although he insisted that nothing had actually happened between them. They split up for a while but he managed to persuade Kate to return and give him another chance. However, he had started to give a colleague a lift to work, a woman who lived nearby, and Kate saw text messages on his phone between them. Again, he said that nothing had taken place, but she did not believe him and this time she left for good. He was devastated and heart-broken, and told me that he had never got over the break-up with Kate. He constantly blamed himself for them splitting up and felt he had ruined his own life. He said he still could not move on from this, 12 years later, and no other woman could ever replace Kate. She was now so idealised in his mind that she had become some kind of goddess. This was even though their relationship had not been totally satisfying, as it was lacking real authenticity, and they did not have a properly shared life.

After Kate left he did in fact start a relationship with the woman he used to give a lift to work. She clearly had strong feelings for him and their relationship was physically passionate, as he appreciated her enthusiasm and love of life, so in contrast to his own "glass half-empty" attitude. This relationship lasted for about two years, but she eventually gave up on him due to his inability to commit to her. He said he had loved her and missed her very much as well. Interestingly, he did not tell me about this relationship until we were well into the therapy, as he felt it might detract from me being fully aware of the devastation he felt when Kate left. However, he knew that withholding this important part of his life was not helpful so he eventually admitted it. If either of these two women were ever mentioned at work, as they were both colleagues, it left him traumatised for weeks, "as though I had been burnt by a red hot poker," as he put it.

His last important relationship was with the woman he accompanied to couples counselling, but this was very on-off and by the time he started to see me, it was "off" again. It lingered on for many months though, as she was deeply in love with him and really wanted it to work. Unfortunately, she was at a great disadvantage by still being under Kate's shadow. James said that he had fallen into the relationship because he warmed to her, as she was so motherly towards him and looked after him, but also because they did connect at a deeper level and he was fully aware of her many attributes. However, this lady was more dominant than his previous partner, and for the first time in his life he found himself arguing with her. He hated confrontation, having had no real experience of it, and therefore never really had to deal with it. Their bickering was something he could not cope with long-term, and this finally decided him not to continue in a romantic relationship with her. Also the physical attraction was not really there for him and although he tried hard to make that less important, of course it did matter. We discussed how it might have worked out if he had settled down with her, as she so wanted, but then met someone who attracted him physically. The pattern of another illicit relationship would start again and he would be back to square one.

James's main concern, however, was the fact that he felt like a scared little child most of the time. He said he had never grown up and his whole life was a house of cards that he had carefully built up, but if one of those cards was pulled away then the whole construct would collapse. He never dared to let the real James be on display as he feared his real self would be unacceptable. He constantly feared the disapproval that he had received from his parents throughout his formative years and was therefore constantly seeking approval. He had never really received unconditional love and been accepted for who he was and so was inhibited to such a degree that he could not show who he really was for fear of judgement and condemnation. He constantly toed the line and conformed to what he thought was expected of him, to the detriment of his inner feelings. Such was his inner conflict that his whole life was nothing but a chore to be worked through until death claimed him and, although he assured me that he would never actually kill himself, death was what he most looked forward to as a way of escaping from his miserable life.

When I questioned James about his parents' background, some fascinating facts emerged. When his father was aged seven, he found his own father dead from a gunshot wound in the woods near their home. James's grandfather had killed himself. His father then had to take on the responsibility of being the man of the house, with one younger sister. He never spoke of this family tragedy and carried the pain and trauma of it with him throughout his life. James said his father relied emotionally on his mother, who had died two years before James came to see me. She had been the third child in her family and the only girl, arriving after the loss of a sister at age four. His mother was a shy and anxious person, and hearing about her family history, one can conjecture that her parents may have been particularly over-protective towards their only daughter, after tragically losing her older sister. Clearly, neither of James's parents was able to contain their own anxieties and so they were unable to teach him how to do so for himself. James therefore grew up feeling that the world was an unsafe and scary place, and it has remained so, despite him managing to carve out a successful career.

When we discussed these things, James said: "I know what is wrong with me but I don't know how to change things. I'm like someone standing on the edge of the swimming pool with everyone telling me to come on in – the water's lovely, but I daren't jump in. However, I *do* jump in and somehow I swim but I don't enjoy it." He reiterated how he could not cope with life, putting on a mask the whole time. He spread his arms wide apart and said, "The James persona that I put on, the one that people see and think I am, is here," and he gestured outwards with one hand, "whilst the real James, the lonely, insecure person who wishes he wasn't a grown up because he can't handle the responsibility and is cripplingly shy, is over here," and he stretched his other hand in the opposite direction, leaving a wide gap in between.

We looked again at how his childhood had left him with feelings of shame and humiliation and of having his confidence and self-esteem eroded on a daily basis through the teasing, belittling and bullying, as well as the expectations that he felt he could never fulfil. He had since developed his professional mask as a way of facing the world and I told him a quote by Winnicott, "It is a joy to be hidden but a disaster not to be found."

I tried giving James various strategies to improve his mood and his self-esteem. Some of them he followed for a short while but not totally consistently. He told me he was "a hard nut to crack" or that he was "a granite man" who needed a lot of chipping away at before there could be any change. We also looked at reasons why he had not mourned his mother properly since her death, despite having once been so close to her. In fact, he had spent the final week of her life looking after her, but left some hours before she died as his brother came to take over her care. Their sister was abroad at the time and felt huge guilt for not having been around when their mother died. When I asked James how he now felt about his mother, he said his predominant feeling was one of resentment as she had not prepared him sufficiently for facing up to life. I suggested he might like to write a letter to his mother expressing all he felt about her. He did this and read it out to me the following week. It was eloquent and poignant and I hoped it might help him to process some of his painful feelings regarding her.

During his childhood, James slowly and painfully learned to suppress his authenticity so as not to displease or upset or anger his parents. As an adult, he paid a terrible price for that suppression. It caused him depression, an inability to trust his own emotions, difficulties in making decisions and, above all, a fear and distrust of the world, making it impossible for him to experience true intimacy with anyone. He longed for it but it also terrified him as he felt he might lose himself, just as Claire (in Chapter 3) used to fear, and be taken over and intruded upon because he had no real sense of autonomy. He did not know how to be himself, alongside another person, and be accepted and welcomed for who he was. I encouraged him to try to be himself but he would always say that no one would want to know the real him; the morose, cynical, depressed man who was so needy and felt like a scared child. He could not seem to acknowledge any of his good points or even realise that he had them.

After about a year of therapy, James had a work meeting which Kate also attended. He knew she would be there and was dreading it. When he next saw me, he told me that it had been an ordeal, as he had to sit next to her in a small room all day, and that she was pregnant at the time. He knew she had married the year before. During the lunch break, he confided in her that he had never got over her and that seeing her was very difficult. She replied that she found that hard to believe – which really angered him. He said that, in some ways, this anger helped him, especially as she was now carrying another man's baby. It brought some kind of closure for him, and stopped him from ever imagining or fantasising that they might one day get back together. About six months later, he heard that the second love of his life, his girlfriend after Kate, was also pregnant. Again, this caused great waves of regret and self-recrimination as that relationship too was now closed off to him forever. When he said that if she had shown at all willing, he would have resumed the relationship, I was confused. She had finished it due to his lack of commitment, so I asked him to explain. He smiled and said, "Well, that's me all over isn't it? I don't know what I've got until it's gone and it's too late, and then I miss it and want it back."

After about 14 months, James decided to take voluntary redundancy from his job, where his hours were erratic and caused problems with his sleep patterns. He had been doing this work for about 25 years and although he had made a success of it, the toll it took on his personal life was proving to be too much. So he decided to have some time off and then start afresh with a new venture. His one-time girlfriend, with whom he had had the on-off long-term relationship, was going to help him set this up and they decided to go into partnership together. He said he felt that, as she now knew he did not want a physical relationship, she would get into bed with him professionally instead of personally. It was a way to keep him close.

During the first few weeks of his redundancy, James became more depressed and pessimistic about his future. Although he now had the chance to catch up on the sleep he felt he had been deprived of for so long, he did not actually sleep that well. He was plagued by nightmares of his two previous girlfriends and often woke up in a state of fear. He found this time of being in limbo almost unbearable and became extremely irritable during our sessions. At the same time, he was coping with the fact that his elderly father had been admitted to hospital after a fall, and was steadily deteriorating. It was decided that he could not be discharged back to his own home, therefore James and his siblings had to organise putting their father into a care home. All this took a toll on James as well.

With some relief to both of us, James started his new venture after three months of not doing very much. It seemed to be going well, apart from the fact that he had constant arguments with his business partner, which exemplified their relationship – as he complained of finding her irrational, over-emotional and capable of twisting facts to suit herself. He was glad that he had not agreed for them to be a couple as she had once wanted.

At this time, I felt that James was under a lot of pressure trying to establish a new business. Therefore, I thought it might be an idea to try and ease that burden by a change of approach. I suggested that instead of endeavouring to change his patterns of behaviour, which was what we had been working on up until then, perhaps he should just accept how he was for the time being, and try to relax and not push himself into social situations or do things that made him feel uncomfortable. Unfortunately, James took enormous exception to this change of tactic. He had already been changing and missing sessions quite regularly and

I knew he was disenchanted with the whole process. Unlike Rick (in Chapter 7), who had fully taken on board that he needed to change the way he tackled people and situations, James seemed unable to make those fundamental shifts. Maybe it all felt too scary to step out of the invisible prison of his own making, as he had hidden behind those high walls for so many years. The strategies I had recommended had been tried for a short time but he never followed them through with any particular enthusiasm. He had read books I had given him that I felt would enlighten him and help him to feel more understood, but nothing seemed to help him to overcome his reluctance to engage more with the world or to reach out to people. He joined a yoga class for a time. He joined a tennis club for a while. He still painted and played the guitar and ran regularly, but these solitary pursuits were the only ones he seemed happy to continue. Anything that involved other people or meaningful change was a step too far. True intimacy was still too painful or scary to contemplate.

After about 18 months, James missed a face-to-face session that I thought we had arranged in his previous Skype session. He said that he had never agreed to come and that he would think about it, but he did not tell me whether he was accepting or not. After another three weeks, he eventually emailed to say he would not be coming again. I was disappointed that he did not discuss this with me and felt that he had done his usual cutting off without any proper explanation. It saddened me that he had behaved so predictably and seemed to think that was all right. I wondered if he might eventually consider that he had done what he usually did, which was to appreciate what he had only once it had gone. I replied to his email telling him how I felt, but said my door was open should he wish to resume the work. It was the only opportunity I had to tell him this, as he had allowed us no chance to talk about his decision, but he clearly took exception to my email as he never replied. Some weeks later, I sent him an article I thought might interest him, on "loneliness", and he thanked me for it, but the last I saw of him was his frozen image at the end of our final Skype session.

The writer Maya Angelou once said, "There is no agony like bearing an untold story inside of you." Although I was ultimately unable to help James move on with his life in the way I would have liked, I still hope that being allowed the time and space to articulate some of his story has helped him to go forward with a better understanding of who he is and how he came to be that way. Maybe in the future, he will be able to reflect on his past and find the courage to make some fundamental changes that will benefit him.

# Chapter 9

# Shadow woman

As Frances deteriorated I threw myself into my work, as a means of release and a distraction from thinking about the terrible way her life was ending. I found it almost unbearable to contemplate. She had moved into a care home, despite being younger than any of the other residents, and it was not easy for her. At first she kept asking to come home, and she became distraught when I explained that this was now her home. I always came away in tears and felt terrible for leaving her there, and yet I knew there was no other option. She needed too much care for one person to undertake. Sometimes she would run down the corridor and grab the hand of another resident who was sitting in a chair and force them to run with her. The staff could not catch her as she was fast. Her behaviour was disturbing the other residents and their relatives began to complain. The first care home eventually told us that her behaviour was too challenging and we needed to find an alternative. After a few extremely anxious weeks, we did find another care home and this proved to be much better than the first one. It had more of a family atmosphere than of an institution.

She seemed to settle there and became friendly with another female resident who had been a physicist but had now lost the power of speech. Frances took her under her wing and referred to her as her "baby". They always sat next to each other at meal times and Frances made sure that her friend had enough to eat, as she could not feed herself.

I used to talk to the other residents during my weekly visits and each one told me about trauma in their childhood, in one form or another. It appeared to be a common denominator and one that never seemed to be explored by doctors or researchers. When Frances was first seen at The National Hospital I gave her consultant a written summary of her early life, which listed the developmental traumas she had undergone, but no one seemed to connect these with her eventual diagnosis.

In time, Frances forgot how to walk and at first I would help her by standing in front of her, holding her hands and encouraging her to walk towards me. We would walk along that way, like a mother teaching her child, but then the day came when she could no longer remember how to stand up – so her walking days were finally over. As our brains control everything we do, once the brain can no longer send out signals to our limbs then those limbs will no longer work. That is one reason why so many dementia patients sit slumped in chairs all day long.

Watching Frances being reduced to a mere shadow of the person she had once been was heartbreaking. The natural end to this tragic story is that one forgets how to swallow and eventually how to breathe. I had hoped that something else would carry her off well before that time, something like a stroke or a heart attack or pneumonia, but it was not to be. She had to endure this dreadful disease right up to its bitter end. I often thought back to one day that was imprinted on my memory while she was living with us. She begged me to kill her as she could not bear living any more. She told me that she was no longer a person and wanted me to put an end to the torture. I could not do it and told her that she *was* still a person and that we all loved her and would look after her and help her. This particular conversation haunted me and I often wondered if I should have just smothered her with a pillow during the night. Of course, I could never have actually done that but sometimes, looking at the ruined shell of the person she had become in those final months, I wished I could have done it. Someone in the final stages of Alzheimer's has been totally hollowed out from inside and there is just a frail body casing around them. The rest has dissolved and disappeared.

Some people's childhoods leave them so vulnerable and unprepared for facing the realities of life. They come from ostensibly loving families, like James (in Chapter 8), but their parents, despite their best intentions, are unable to provide them with that bedrock of safety and stability, or inner security, which would allow them to flourish as an adult. The lifelong habits of hiding their feelings and never speaking of emotional issues, but skirting round them to avoid upsetting anyone or letting anyone know the truth of how they feel inside, leave children unable to access their own emotional lives and the essence of their innermost feelings. This is, in fact, a form of traumatic experience for we are all hard-wired to seek attachment with those nearest to us. If that attachment is constantly thwarted and made to feel wrong, then the child grows to adulthood without being able to express themselves, and constantly feels that they are inadequate and wanting in some deep fundamental way. They often develop lifelong insecurities about themselves and the world in general. This is how it was with Eleanor.

# Eleanor

Eleanor described herself as a "shadow woman". The reason she saw herself that way was because she had come under the powerful influence of a teacher as a young child – a ballet teacher. This teacher was a "puppet master" par excellence and had dominated and manipulated her pupil's life for decades. Eleanor said that, whatever she did, she felt she was controlled by this woman and thus was her "shadow", moving in concert with her and following her every move with no will of her own. She spent her life living in the shadows, uncomfortable with her body and unable to live a fulfilling life.

Eleanor swung like a pendulum between her mother, who she described as "a simmering pot", and her ballet teacher. As she grew up she was so used to being manipulated and "stage-managed" that she attracted men in her life who continued the manipulation. The pattern felt so familiar to her that she kept repeating it. Each time she managed to extricate herself from one manipulative relationship she would fall into another one. After the break-up of each relationship she felt guilty, particularly about all the mistakes she had made with men. This is what led her to marry a man she did not really love. She thought he was a good person who had suffered from a raw deal in life, and that it was her duty to look after him and try to make him happy. She also saw it as a kind of penance for all her previous failures and what she perceived to be weaknesses and poor judgements on her part. This marriage would be her way of compensating for all the bad things she felt she had done so far.

Of course, the marriage faltered and eventually ground to a halt. Eleanor's husband had always put her on a pedestal and could hardly believe his luck when she agreed to marry him. However, once he had her up on that pedestal he kept her there, isolated and lonely. He made her distance herself from her friends, saying he did not like them and they were not good enough for her. He insisted that she was not up to entertaining and would criticise her cooking if she did invite people over, so she eventually gave up trying to entertain and began to believe him. She discovered that he was mean, so they hardly ever went out; except on a Sunday he might take her for tea at a local garden centre, like an elderly married couple instead of newly-weds.

Eleanor became depressed and exhausted with the struggle of maintaining the illusion of a happily married couple. After six years she managed to leave the marriage, but he prevaricated so much around the divorce that it took another four years before that was finalised. By the end of the marriage, Eleanor felt defeated and had lost any self-esteem she may have had. Her husband had managed to make her feel worthless – and yet she had the perseverance and drive to leave him and make a new life for herself.

Eleanor first came to see me around 18 months before her divorce came through. She had met a new man some months earlier and he was in therapy for many problems. He recognised that she too had numerous issues and suggested she should also seek therapy.

Eleanor started by explaining that she came from a family where feelings were not discussed – in fact, they were swept under the carpet to such a degree that even when people were in dire need of help, they were ignored. Eleanor had suffered from eating disorders throughout her adolescence and early 20s, primarily due to the malign influence of her ballet teacher. Her teacher had told pupils, when they reached puberty and their bodies began to fill out a little, that now was the time for them to stop eating. She suggested they skip their evening meals and eat an apple instead. At around this time, Eleanor was shown a film at school about eating disorders, as a warning in order to prevent them; however, she learnt about bulimia from watching this film and decided this would be a brilliant way to keep her weight under control. She was friendly with another ballet student who taught her how to make herself vomit. She first became anorexic and then bulimic. She said that when she was in the grip of bulimia, she would go to the bathroom to make herself sick and family members would hear her but no one ever said a word about it. Fortunately, she had managed to deal with this problem in a previous therapy, but it hovered around her nevertheless and her eating habits were strange.

Eleanor had an older brother and a younger sister. She had always looked up to her brother, somewhat idolising him. She had a prickly relationship with her sister – who she felt was favoured by their mother. At the same time, Eleanor readily admitted to having been her father's favourite. Apart from her eating habits, Eleanor had problems with her sleep, extreme shyness and an inability to be on time. The latter difficulty seemed to be a learned behaviour from her family, who were traditionally always late, and it almost seemed to be a badge of honour among them all.

After leaving her marriage, Eleanor went to live in a tiny studio flat and continued with her work as a dance teacher. She had followed her teacher's path and now ran her own little school, having worked for years helping to run her teacher's school – often for very low pay. After some time on her own, she realised she needed therapy to help her with the way her disastrous marriage had made her feel and so she found someone who seemed ideal. Unfortunately, this therapy only added to her troubles, as the therapist manipulated her in the worst possible way and after two years she was left in an even worse state. She managed to extricate herself but was still not divorced, as her soon-to-be ex-husband prevaricated and delayed the process. Some months before coming to see me she started a relationship with a young man with whom she fell deeply in love. He was already in therapy and quickly saw how much she needed help too – so he asked his therapist to recommend someone for Eleanor, and that is how I first came to see her.

At the beginning of her therapy with me, Eleanor seemed like someone completely defeated by life. She was still in thrall to her all-powerful teacher, who dominated her life to a frightening degree. Although Eleanor could now see that this person did not really have her best interests at heart, she still felt a loyalty towards her teacher – preventing her from breaking away and finishing what was in reality an unhealthy relationship. It took some years of therapy before Eleanor was able to distance herself sufficiently from her teacher to establish a better pattern of living. She eventually began to see her for who she was, and form a realistic appraisal of how much damage this woman had wrought in her life so far.

At the other end of the spectrum, Eleanor was also still dependent upon the approval of her mother who vacillated between being over-protective and harshly dismissive. Her mother sometimes banished her for weeks at a time, refusing to have anything to do with her, due to some perceived slight towards her on Eleanor's part. Negotiating this complex relationship took up a lot of Eleanor's energy and often left her exhausted. Her relationships with her older brother and younger sister were equally complex and old family patterns were played out time and again. Her father, to whom she felt the closest bond, often exasperated her – this relationship too was very "up and down".

Eleanor's friendships were spasmodic; her one true friend from childhood was married with two young children and no longer seemed to care enough about their friendship to take any real interest in Eleanor's life, as she was so taken up with her own interests. Other friends tended to drop by the wayside as Eleanor was too shy to pick up the phone and keep in touch, so would often wait until they contacted her. Friendships cannot survive such neglect and so she had gradually lost many old friends. She did have contacts with old boyfriends. These often proved to be more trouble than they were worth.

Although Eleanor was in a relationship with a young man who she felt she loved, he had considerable problems of his own. She tried to help him as best she could and he relied on her for many things, but could never actually give her the love she craved – because he was too damaged himself. His needs were even greater than hers and so he used her kind nature and generosity to look after himself whilst taking advantage of her. She was like a little bird in a cage. The door to the cage was open but she could never fly out. It was safer to stay inside and look out and wish for the freedom that was in fact hers, but that she could not grasp.

At first the therapy concentrated on Eleanor's family background and relationships, covering her difficulties in establishing and maintaining female friendships and her propensity to become involved with men who manipulated her. We also had to tackle her strange eating and sleeping habits, her chronic shyness, which prevented her from socialising or even going out to buy clothes, and her fraught interactions with members of her family.

Some months after beginning therapy, Eleanor's relationship with her boyfriend began to falter. She started to see how much he used her, even to the extent of inviting himself to accompany her on a holiday she had arranged, which she let him do, paying for it all out of her own limited funds. Fairly soon after this he broke off the relationship, leaving her, once again, bereft and heartbroken. For some months afterwards he kept in irregular contact and used her when he needed somewhere to stay and be looked after, for instance, while he was recovering from an operation. He owed her money from the holiday he had joined her on and never paid her back. Eventually, she saw him for the manipulator he really was and learnt from the experience, although it saddened her deeply.

Gradually, Eleanor learned to be more resilient in the face of the relentless bullying by her old dance teacher, with whom she still had professional contact. She also learned to protect herself when others used her to their own advantage and even managed to say "no" on occasion, whereas in the past she would have done anything to ensure that the other person thought well of her. She tentatively accepted that how she behaved and reacted might not be the way that others would behave and react. This is always such a hard lesson for anyone to learn. Her relationships with her mother and siblings began to improve, even when her mother would do her usual trick of refusing to speak to her after some imagined slight. Eleanor just sat it out until her mother relented and their relationship adjusted again, whereas in the past she might have prolonged the argument or maintained the silence so that things became even more strained and difficult.

Although her work as a dance teacher did not bring in much money, Eleanor was able to supplement it with examining; she enjoyed this aspect of her work as it allowed her to travel a bit and to meet new people. This, in itself, reinforced her confidence when she realised that others warmed to her and she found that she was not as socially inept as she thought. She now had a slightly higher profile in the world of dance examinations and was invited to events that in the past she had not attended. One of the older male examiners took a liking to her and would invite her out socially. She enjoyed these occasions although she knew that this was not a romantic relationship, as he was much older than her. He was unmarried and she deduced that he was lonely and found her company agreeable – so was happy to go along with it, as she liked him and it gave her an opportunity to socialise without anxiety.

It took a few years before Eleanor began to feel free of the shackles that her marriage and her past relationships had fastened round her. The chains gradually loosened and the huge burden of guilt she had carried with her over the years, for her perception of having spoiled things throughout her life, began to dissolve. Talking through many painful episodes in her life allowed her the distance and perspective to see that she had not always been the one at fault and that often blame lay at other people's doors. She could now see clearly that many people had taken her good nature for granted and that she had fallen into many traps over the years, but was now more aware of how those snares had been set and could take steps to avoid them in the future.

Eleanor's work is still ongoing but she now has a different approach to life. Although life is still hard for her and she does not find it easy to go out happily into the world, she does at least venture forth. She steps out of the cage, flies a short distance and then comes back to the safety of the world she has created for herself. Hopefully, in time, she will feel as safe in the outside world as she does within her invisible cage.

Eleanor now spaces out her therapy sessions, so she only visits me about once a month and this seems sufficient to keep her stable. She has also looked at the possibility of taking on extra part-time work in order to supplement her income as a dance teacher and examiner. This would expand her world even further and maybe allow her to meet other people removed from the stifling world of dance that has been her social milieu for so long. She has stepped out tentatively into the world that in the past seemed like a place that was not for her, that she could not negotiate or move around in easily. After years of therapy, she has learned to rely on herself more and not trust others to the same extent as in the past. Eleanor now seems to appreciate that she has the right to inhabit this world and play her part in it. She has stepped out from the shadows and now walks in daylight.

# Chapter 10

# Conclusions

After Frances died, I felt a huge mixture of emotions. Of course, I was heartbroken at losing my only sister, even though I had effectively lost her to Alzheimer's years before she died. At the same time, I was relieved that the suffering was over for her. During the long years of her illness I wrote the following prose poem about how I viewed what was happening to us:

*Drowning in the Lonely Sea of Forgetting*

We are both in the water together.
You are holding me tightly with your arms clasped around me.
We are swimming together.

Gradually your hold loosens and you start to slip further into the water.
I try to hold you but your grip is not firm. I realise you are going under.
I try to keep you above water and sometimes you bob up and see me clearly.
Then the water covers you again.
Eventually you no longer come to the surface.
I see you clearly, under the water, but out of reach.

I often think of how much suffering people have to endure and how it could be alleviated in so many ways, if people were just kinder to each other and showed compassion to each other. Kindness is a much under-rated virtue and it is one that I have tried to nurture and cultivate in my sons.

I now have three grandchildren and watch them grow with great love and pride. Grandchildren are for me truly the best part of being a parent as you can watch your child become a parent and do things for their children that you know they have learnt from their own upbringing. The grandchildren themselves are always wondrous and wonderful as they are so open to everything, so curious and inventive and loving. One can also once again see the world through a child's eyes and that is a joy, as everything becomes new and amazing as you visualise everything afresh, bathed in the light of total innocence, untainted by your own world-weary experiences.

It is those world-weary experiences that have shaped the people that I have seen in therapy, some of whom I have been able to help. I know there are others whose therapies have not been entirely successful but I hope that they will still have learnt some useful things from their therapy experience.

I also hope that the soul stories I have shared here have been illuminating and that reading them may inspire other therapists – or may help other people who are going through problems of their own to consider therapy. Each story is always unique and individual, and every person I see brings different insights into how attachment-based therapy is so relevant in today's world. It is the first five years of a child's life that shapes how that child will respond to the world thereafter. As Wordsworth so eloquently put it in his *Intimations of Immortality* – "The child is father to the man" and that is as true now as when he first wrote it.

It still surprises me that some people come for therapy and do not wish to explore their childhood. They say things like, "Well, I know I didn't have a happy childhood but it's in the past now. I want to get on with my life and look to the future. I want to move on from that." I have to explain to them that they can only expect to move on once they understand how they came to be where they are. To understand that, they need to know what shaped them, what made them respond to the world the way they do and what makes them react to people and their actions now. It is all rooted in their first few years.

It is all very well to offer people cognitive behavioural therapy (CBT) but that will do nothing to touch deep-rooted problems that impact one's very sense of self. CBT uses only the rational brain and trains you to think in a different way and so is fine for some phobias, recent anxieties, mild depression and minor bouts of psychological disturbance; fear of flying or public speaking, for instance. It cannot train you to feel differently though. Emotions run much deeper than thoughts and are inextricably bound up with our earliest memories. When it comes to debilitating depression or overwhelming anxiety it has now been found that people who underwent CBT for such problems, five years ago or longer, and appeared to have been helped at the time, have since regressed and found that their depression or anxiety has returned. People who underwent deep psychotherapy, on the other hand, usually remain more stable and less liable to regress. This is because they have not just had their symptoms treated temporarily *but the cause of their problems treated* and so the problem does not recur – if it has been successfully addressed, processed and worked through. It is a much longer process and a more painful process, but is worthwhile in the end.

The root of any psychotherapy, whatever the mode of treatment, is the relationship between the therapist and the patient. It is this bond and special form of communication that makes therapy work, when it does work. When a therapist shows compassion and empathy and really listens to the person she (or he) is working with, then there is a good chance that healing can take place. Therapists who talk down to their patients, think they know best or dismiss their patient's deepest feelings are unlikely to have successful outcomes. It is essential that patients have trust in their therapists, particularly since most people who come for therapy have had their trust shattered in one way or another from earliest childhood. The root of all psychological disturbance is trauma and it is the trauma that needs to be uncovered and treated before any healing can begin. Trauma can take many forms but the most insidious occurs in families that from the outside appear to be loving and containing but in reality are far from that. When parents cannot meet the emotional needs of their children then the children suffer trauma from their unmet needs. This trauma stays with them throughout life, unless it is addressed and processed in a loving way with a sympathetic witness. That is the essence of psychotherapy.

The few examples I have written about in this book have been an attempt to show how a variety of psychological disturbances can be treated by the patient being listened to, being allowed to share their story with someone empathic and having their experiences validated and understood. We are all relational creatures and our need for attachment is universal. When those attachments are broken, disrupted or perverted, we need help and the only way to help those with attachment problems is to introduce and build a safe attachment in the form of the therapeutic relationship, if no other close relationship is available.

I finish this book by expressing my love and gratitude for my own close relationships with my husband, Barry, and our two sons, Matthew and Laurence. I am also deeply thankful for the kindness, patience, humour and wisdom of my wonderful circle of female friends. Lastly I am, of course, indebted to the unique and vulnerable patients I have seen over the years.

# References

Bloom, William (2011) *The Endorphin Effect: A breakthrough strategy for holistic health and spiritual wellbeing,* Piatkus.

Bowlby, John (1997) *Attachment and Loss,* Pimlico.

Cusk, Rachel (2002) *A Life's Work: On Becoming A Mother,* Fourth Estate.

Duffell, Nick (2000) *The Making of Them: The British Attitude to Children and the Boarding School System,* Lone Arrow Press.

Eppel, Alan (2009) *Sweet Sorrow: Love, Loss and Attachment in Human Life,* Karnac Books.

Fernyhough, Charles (2012) *Pieces of Light: The new science of memory,* Profile Books.

Kohut, Heinz (1966) *Forms and Transformations of Narcissism,* Sage Journals.

Kohut, Heinz (2009) *The analysis of the self: A systematic approach to the psychoanalytic treatment of narcissistic personality disorders,* University of Chicago Press.

James, Oliver (2012) *Love Bombing: Reset Your Child's Emotional Thermostat,* Karnac Books.

Levine, Peter (1997) *Waking The Tiger: Healing Trauma,* North Atlantic Books.

Loyd, Alex and Johnson, Ben (2011) *The Healing Code,* Grand Central Life & Style.

Lomas, Peter (2000) Chapter 2 in *Doing Good?: Psychotherapy out of its Depth,* Oxford University Press.

Siegel, Daniel (2020) *The Developing Mind: How Relationships and the Brain interact to shape who we are,* Guilford Press.

174

Weil, Simone (2009) In *Waiting on God*, Routledge.

White, Kate, Cotter, Angela and Leventhal, Hazel (2018) *Dementia: An Attachment Approach*, Routledge.

Winnicott, Donald (1953) *Transitional objects and transitional phenomena*, International Journal of Psychoanalysis 34, 89-97.

Winnicott, Donald (2017) *Transitional objects and transitional phenomena* in *The Collected Works of D. W. Winnicott: Volume 9, 1969 – 1971*, Oxford University Press.

www.ingramcontent.com/pod-product-compliance
Lightning Source LLC
Chambersburg PA
CBHW072246270326
41930CB00010B/2286